JOINING THE DANCE

A Theology of the Spirit

JOINING THE DANCE

A Theology of the Spirit

Molly T. Marshall

JUDSON PRESS • VALLEY FORGE

JOINING THE DANCE
A Theology of the Spirit

Judson Press has made every effort to trace the ownership of all quotes. In the event of a question arising from the use of a quote, we regret any error made and will be pleased to make the necessary correction in future printings and editions of this book.

Direct Bible quotations in this volume are from the New Revised Standard Version of the Bible, copyright© 1989 by the Division of Christian Education of the National Council of the Churches of Christ in the United States of America. Used by permission. All rights reserved. On occasion the author, Molly T. Marshall, provides her own translation, especially when it makes the language for God more inclusive. In those instances, the Bible reference appears outside of quotations.

Library of Congress Cataloging-in-Publication Data

Marshall, Molly Truman.
Joining the dance : a theology of the Spirit / Molly T. Marshall.
    p. cm.
Includes bibliographical references.
    ISBN 0-8170-1413-6 (pbk. : alk. paper)
1. Holy Spirit. I.Title.
BT121.3.M27 2003
231'.3--dc21

2002040574

Printed in the U.S.A.
09 08 07 06 05 04 03

10 9 8 7 6 5 4 3 2 1

To the *Communio Sanctorum*
at Central Baptist Theological Seminary

CONTENTS

FOREWORD

MANY OF US READ BOTH ACADEMIC AND POPULAR BOOKS IN ORDER
to stimulate our theological reflections, yet often we come away
after reading the last page and closing the cover with a sense that
something was missing in the words. Most of us attempt to live
Christian lives, yet in the daily rhythms sometimes a sense of the
thinness of participation occurs. Instead of experiencing the fullness of Christian faith, we have shallow encounters that reveal
how pavid our experiences truly are. We may be unable, or perhaps more accurate to say, unwilling to figure out what is lacking, but we have sensed it. Like an empty chair at the table or a
loved one absent from a family picture, incompleteness is felt.
Awkwardly, we continue moving to the music that springs from
our Bibles and religious traditions, but we glide along alone
across the dance floor for lack of a partner.

Molly Marshall has sensed and named the missing partner; it
is the Spirit. While much contemporary theological writing
focuses a spotlight upon the waltzing of God and Christ, the
Spirit has been relegated to one of the chairs along the wall of the
ballroom. Marshall, always with an eye upon the life of the community of faith, writes that the dance is not complete unless the
Spirit—the One who empowers our dancing—leads.

Dancing is the image Marshall uses to reclaim the importance
of the Spirit in theology today. It is an appropriate image that
describes the role of the Spirit and how the Spirit functions in a
non-hierarchical and a non-patriarchal way within the triune
God, both important points for Marshall's work. For Marshall
the image of dance also represents a call for all of us to realize
that we also can participate, along with all creation, in the Spirit
who pulls us into the life of God. Or as Marshall writes, "Never

static, the Spirit is God's enlivening action, both within the triune God and encompassing all that God has made. Through vivifying, gathering, empowering, birthing, transforming, winnowing, and honoring, the Spirit forges a partnership between God and all creation that brings both divine and creaturely being to the ultimate realization of participation" (p. 160). Perhaps one of the most helpful contributions from Marshall's theology of the Spirit is how she opens readers' eyes to see the tangible places where the Spirit is creatively participating in life.

For those seeking a scriptural basis for this emphasis on the Spirit, they will be well pleased with Marshall's insightful reading of Scripture. She provides a biblical bedrock for a theology of the Spirit by demonstrating the prominence of the Spirit in the biblical witness and the surprising ways in which the Spirit dances through Scripture. The author not only exegetes Scripture, but she also deftly exegetes contemporary culture, society, and church in order to provide a pneumatology that is holistic and relevant.

Marshall also takes old voices from the early church and new voices from contemporary theologians and combines them into a chorus whose song illustrates the continuing task of interpreting the Spirit. From the old voices, a reader will note that this book is liberally sprinkled with Latin and Greek words, phrases, and images. These represent the rich but often neglected heritage of the early mothers and fathers of the church. The author's use of these words, phrases, and images illustrates that our ancestors in faith also sought to find ways to speak about the Spirit as they attempted to participate within the life of God. Marshall helps us renew our often trite and shallow contemporary Christian language with the ancient vocabulary of faith that sustained our ancestors for two millennia.

Not only old voices, but also new voices are heard in Marshall's theology. The author's engagement with female and male theologians, drawn from a variety of ethnicities, denominations, religious traditions, and backgrounds, reflects the participatory model that Marshall sees as critical for life in the Spirit. She engages the contemporary reflections of these major theological thinkers, and she incorporates their thoughtful insights while judiciously critiquing their points of weakness.

To read this theology of the Spirit calls forth participation on behalf of the reader. It is a heart-given invitation to participate in the life of the Spirit. So perhaps the most fitting words with which to begin your reading are the ones uttered by John the Seer: "The Spirit and the Bride say, 'Come'" (Revelation 22:17).

David M. May
Professor of New Testament
Central Baptist Theological Seminary
Kansas City, Kansas

PREFACE

WRITING A TEXT ON PNEUMATOLOGY IS UNDOUBTEDLY THE MOST daunting challenge I have ever taken up. The biblical metaphors are plentiful, but elusive. The writings of early Christianity "stumble in the right direction,"[1] in the words of Kilian McDonnell, but there is much more to say. Interest in the Spirit is always part of a larger christological or Trinitarian concern, and one is easily drawn aside. Not only are there many possibilities for heresy (of which I daily grow more aware), but also there is an ineffable mystery to the subject.

While this book seeks to articulate fresh insights about the Spirit in my voice, it is hardly an objective or solitary project— many voices echo in these pages. There is the sound of a fine silence (1 Kings 19:12), the voice of the Spirit. One writes about the Spirit only in the power of the Spirit; one discerns the mode of God's presence as Spirit only because of the revealing presence within one's deepest self, in the context of community. Such work has a reflexive quality that is inescapable and comforting. Many scholarly and ecclesial voices resound here also, from whom I have learned much. And the voices of students, who remain my teachers, offer their lively contributions.

In this book my mind has been drawn toward questions that disturb, that defy easy resolution. Is the sign of the Spirit's presence always harmony, gathering and uniting what is separated and divided; or could division and dispersal be the work of the Spirit? Is unanimity in the body of Christ evidence of the Spirit's leading; or are the pockets of resistance and conflict the places where the Spirit is moving? Do all persons have an intrinsic experience of the Spirit; or is the Spirit the gift that is given only in baptism? Is the Spirit confined to human beings; or does all created reality share in the pulse of the divine life of the Holy Spirit?

Is the abiding Spirit the express presence of the risen Christ; or is the Spirit a unique expression of the being of God? Vexing questions, these—"far beyond our seeing," in the words of Brian Wren's "Bring Many Names."[2]

Each day as I began writing, I prayed the words of the ancient hymn *Veni Creator Spiritus* ("Come, Holy Spirit"), invoking the Spirit's presence as I sought to write faithfully and truthfully. Most days I felt insufficient for the task, but I am cheered by Aslan's words to Prince Caspian: "If you felt yourself sufficient for the task, it would be the proof that you were not." I am encouraged by the words of Hilary, bishop of Poitiers in the fourth century, who knew well the difficulty of words about the Third Person: "Concerning the Holy Spirit, we should neither be silent nor should we speak. But we cannot remain silent because of those people who do not know."[3] I am exhorted not to stint by St. Basil the Great: "Let us not be afraid of being too extravagant in what we say about the Holy Spirit...Our thoughts will always fall short."[4]

The challenge of constructive work on the Spirit was made easier by the two contexts in which this book was written. I began it while a resident scholar at the Institute for Ecumenical and Cultural Research in Collegeville, Minnesota, during the fall of 2000. There could be no better location to pursue this study than a monastery whose very life is shaped by prayer in the Spirit, the rhythms of the *opus Dei*, "to which nothing is to be preferred," as the *Rule of St. Benedict* puts it. There could be no more conducive setting than the stunning beauty of lakes and woods filled with creatures furiously preparing for winter, all vivified by the vital breath of God. I cannot imagine more supportive friends than those in residence at the Institute: Sr. Dolores Schuh, C.H.M. and Fr. Wilfred Theisen, O.S.B., whose lives bear the graceful presence of God's Spirit. I am especially grateful to Dr. Patrick Henry, executive director of the Institute, who read early drafts of several chapters and offered expert editorial advice.

These effects of the Spirit beckoned and sustained my scholarly work while I was there.

Four times a day I experienced the grace of singing in the monks' choir, often praising the work of the Spirit through the hymnody. But we never lingered long there; the liturgy hastened to anchor the Spirit in the safe harbor of the Trinity lest we make the Spirit too much the object of our worship or theological reflection. And there is wisdom in this. "Object" is precisely what the Spirit cannot be, for closer to us than we are to ourselves (*interior intimo meo*) is the divine presence, as St. Augustine noted.

The second half of this book was written in a small cubicle in the library of Central Baptist Theological Seminary in Kansas City, Kansas, where I teach. I spent so much time there during the summer of 2002 that one student called me the "anchoress" of the library. I am hardly St. Julian *redivivus*, but I am grateful for the kindness of the dean, James Hines, the librarian, Donald Keeney, and the library staff for offering this anchorage in which to work and for providing much helpful assistance.

There are other institutions to thank. Material in chapters 2, 6, and 8 comprised portions of the Ingram Lectures offered at Memphis Theological Seminary and the Scott Lectures offered at Brite Divinity School. Material from chapters 1, 2, and 6 was a part of the Spring 2001 Lectures of the Baptist Studies House at Duke Divinity School. I am grateful to these theological schools for the careful hearing and questioning of many ideas now further refined.

Many persons have been integral to the completion of this work. Dean James Hines and President Tom Clifton, as well as the Board of Directors of Central Seminary, enthusiastically supported my sabbatical work, much needed time for research and writing. My colleagues, particularly David May and Mike Graves, read portions of the manuscript and gave thoughtful critique. My colleague Connie McNeill and my friend Luda Teterina indulged me by listening with care to long sections of this text. My graduate assistant, Jerrod H. Hugenot, has done yeoman's duty in overseeing many of the technical details of the process. He not only hunted down numerous sources and corrected errant citations, but also carefully read the manuscript many times over and offered perceptive theological insights and critique. I dare say it would not have been completed without his industry and personal interest. These few words of gratitude fall short of the great indebtedness I feel.

The hardest part of writing this preface is adequately thanking those who have been the nearest midwives in helping birth this book. Douglas Green, my spouse and friend and abiding encourager, has cheered every step along the way. James Hines has been unflagging in his interest and support—excellent qualities in an academic dean! Kerry Campbell and Angela Lowe, dear sisters and friends and colleagues in ministry, have been constant in their care, "walking the mile and bearing the load" in ways that they alone know.

Finally, I desire that this monograph be a prayerful oblation for the good of the people of God, and that in all things, even this, God might be glorified—*In Omnibus Glorificetur Deus*.[5]

Molly T. Marshall
Kansas City, Kansas
Season after Pentecost, 2002

NOTES

1. Kilian McDonnell, "A Trinitarian Theology of the Holy Spirit?" *Theological Studies* 46 (1985): 193–194.

2. This hymn is found in a collection of the same title, *Bring Many Names* (Carol Stream, Ill.: Hope Publishing Company, 1989).

3. *On the Trinity*, cited in McDonnell, "Trinitarian Theology," 199.

4. Cited in Elizabeth A. Johnson, *Women, Earth, and Creator Spirit* (Mahwah, N.J.: Paulist Press, 1993), 51.

5. This is the motto of the Benedictines, drawn from 1 Peter 4:11, quoted in chapter 57 of the *Rule of St. Benedict*. It appears in abbreviated form, "I.O.G.D." on a tower of one of the early buildings at St. John's Abbey and University, Collegeville, Minnesota.

CHAPTER 1

RECOVERING THE SPIRIT

We have not even heard that there is a Holy Spirit.
—Acts 19:2

HE SAT IN THE BACK ROW OF THE VERY FIRST CLASS IN SYSTEMATIC theology. I, as a newly minted Ph.D., tried to articulate my emerging understanding of the traditional theological categories. To my efforts he offered a plaintive refrain: "But what about the Holy Spirit?" I assured him that we would get to that, maybe next semester. As the course developed and I barely managed to stay a lecture ahead of the students, I became aware that I did not know where to place pneumatology, the doctrine concerned with the Holy Spirit. It belonged everywhere—and nowhere. Following the pattern of the Apostles' Creed, I did not address this doctrine until after Christology. My treatment was almost an afterthought, truncated and thoroughly subordinationist. The Spirit came off little better than the stealth weapon of the church, able to convict us of sin and teach us more about Jesus. "What about the Holy Spirit?" indeed!

Another question shapes this study. As a seminary professor I am often in churches for special conferences, seeking to share theological insights with persons who have no formal theological education. At the beginning of a renewal conference focusing on Christian spirituality, I asked those in attendance to write down their questions about the Spirit. One honest soul wrote, "Can the Holy Spirit make you do weird things?" The perception lodged in this question is revealing. Thus is the Spirit caricatured among many, even the biblically literate. Many sound like certain of the

1

Ephesians who, when asked by Paul if they had received the Spirit upon their profession of belief, responded, "We have not even heard that there is a Holy Spirit" (Acts 19:2). Their response is echoed too often today.

The varied terminology does not make things easier. The Bible speaks of the Spirit of God, the Spirit, the Holy Spirit, and spirit—this last term being used of both the divine and the human. At times, Scripture uses personal images such as comforter and teacher; Scripture also uses natural elements such as water, wind, and fire to describe the function or presence of the Spirit. Sorting out the different names and depictions will be necessary as we engage the biblical mosaic and move from that rhetorical field to theological construction.

Both intellectual heritage and theological interpretations have conspired against understanding Spirit as the mode of God's presence in the world, the life-giving power in which all participate. From the Greeks we learn that materiality is a hindrance to spirit; echoing our theological forebears, we accent the transcendent power of God at the expense of the vulnerable nearness of immanent Spirit. From the Rationalists and Vitalists we inherit a worldview that separates the personal nature of God from the etherlike life force described as Spirit; from contemporary "spiritual" writers we hear of the dispensability of God—that is, one can be "spiritual" without presupposing the address of divine being.

The deep sigh of the church is for a renewed awareness of the work of the Spirit in our lives and in this fragile world. Somehow we know that a better understanding of the Spirit holds a key to deepening our relationship with God and our perseverance in faith, hope, and love. We also trust that pneumatology can bridge—or at least blur—the sacred-secular divide that has plagued Christian theology. Yet the mysterious, listing Spirit evades easy systematization; uncontrollable as wind, its currents shape the contours of heart and habitation without our knowing "where it comes from or where it goes" (John 3:8). Tracking the biblical and historical development of pneumatology can evoke trepidation, hence our lack of surefootedness in tracing the labyrinthine pattern.

Regulating, suppressing, and ordering have too often been the church's response to the lively and unpredictable movement of the Spirit. Fearing excessive claims—and there have been many from Corinth to Toronto—theologians have wanted to avoid "swallowing the Spirit, feathers and all,"[1] as Luther accused Karlstadt, a theological nemesis, of doing. The irritant of "enthusiasm" has seemed heretical, even when not officially declared to be so, and consequently the Third Article of the Apostles' Creed has been neglected, contributing to a listless Christianity. My own Baptist tradition, fearing charismatic currents, has offered little comprehensive reflection in pneumatology.[2] The fecundity of the Spirit's work has been rendered sterile, impersonal, and mostly insignificant in a religious tradition ever seeking finer precision, ironically, in what it means to be "born again."

Clearly, there are many reasons why the Holy Spirit still is, sixteen centuries after Gregory of Nazianzus coined the term, the *theos agraptos*, the God about whom nobody writes.[3] The preeminent reason today is that most contemporary Christians are insufficiently Trinitarian. The relational grounding for a robust theology of the Spirit is lacking. This is changing, however. Considerable attention is being given to Trinitarian construction[4] these days, though the implications for pneumatology have not yet been sufficiently addressed. Only a Trinitarian doctrine of the Spirit can be sufficiently encompassing,[5] for it integrates the creative and redemptive work of God. The typical Western theology has tended to stress salvation to the neglect of wider concerns; thus the work of the Spirit has been severely constricted, at least in interpretation. We know down deep, however, that the Spirit cannot be contained by human words, actions, or even all of creation. Spirit

3

is always moving ahead, drawing us to new life and receptivity to God's presence with us.

COMPOSING THE RHYTHM

Kilian McDonnell updates Gregory: "Anyone writing on pneumatology is hardly burdened by the past."[6] This is particularly true in the West. The Eastern church, historically, has made more room for the Spirit in theological formulations[7] and, more importantly, in worship. Maybe the West's reticence can be ascribed to the preoccupation with Christology, or to the elusive and indirect nature of the Spirit's functioning, or simply to the subordination of this member of the Trinity because of doctrinal controversy and creedal missteps. More than a few theologians suggest that the Spirit has been neglected because of the traditional association with the feminine dimension of God. Elizabeth Johnson contends that in recent years, the "theory has grown that one of the key if unarticulated reasons for the tradition's forgetfulness of the Spirit lies...in the alliance between the idea of the Spirit and the roles and persons of actual women marginalized in church and society."[8] All of these reasons are interrelated.[9]

Pneumatology carries considerable promise for addressing concerns central to Christians: the character of God, caring for the groaning creation, the meaning of history, and the agency of God in creaturely life—concerns shared by persons who pursue other ways of faith. A few perceptive texts concerning the nature and function of the Holy Spirit have been published in recent years,[10] some with feminist sensibilities,[11] yet further work is needed. I hope to offer a new vision that will assist the constructive as well as the pastoral function of Christian doctrine.[12]

A new paradigm in pneumatology has not yet emerged, says Jürgen Moltmann. Nonetheless, there are beginnings, and Moltmann is right when he adds that we are witnessing a

4

transition from an anthropocentric to a holistic pneumatology, one that embraces the whole creation and recognizes in the Spirit the symbol of wholeness, relatedness, energy, and life.[13] In his magisterial "contributions to systematic theology" over the past thirty years, Moltmann again and again has returned to the schism between Eastern and Western churches in 1054 over the *filioque* clause.[14] He perceives that the West's stealthy addition to the Creed of Constantinople at the Third Synod of Toledo in 589[15] significantly diminished the encompassing range of the Spirit's working.[16] Others disagree, seeing this modification, which made the function of the Spirit "essentially subservient and instrumental to the work of the incarnate Christ,"[17] as necessary to guard against "the danger of an undefined, unregulated, and, in the final count, unevangelical spirituality."[18]

This fear of "unregulated" pneumatology erupted when Korean theologian Chung Hyun Kyung addressed the World Council of Churches Assembly in Canberra in 1991.[19] This was the first assembly to focus on the Spirit, the first that phrased its theme as a prayer: "Come Holy Spirit—Renew the Whole Creation."[20] After inviting the participants to remove their shoes, because they would be journeying with her toward the holy ground,[21] Chung began to dance and pray, calling upon the spirits of the people (departed and present) to voice "the cries of creation and cries of the Spirit within it."[22] She called to the spirits of Hagar and Jephthah's daughters, of Jewish holocaust victims and those killed at Hiroshima, of the Amazon rain forest and all creation raped for money, of "the Liberator, our brother Jesus, tortured and killed on the cross."[23] After her prayer, she burned the list of names and began her interpretation of the meeting's theme.

Provocative and perceptive, Professor Chung provided a lively beginning to the assembly. One witness reports, "Plenary conversation broke out immediately. 'Syncretism!' cried one Orthodox bishop....'Diversity,' 'cultural and religious pluralism,' replied

'Third World' voices."[24] Another observer remarked that following Chung's presentation "there was passionate applause, but there was also passionate silence."[25] It seems that a great deal of the negative reaction was over Chung's generic use of spirit and the relating of the Holy Spirit to creation.[26] Her identification of the movement of the Spirit with the cries of the oppressed and her bold call for repentance unnerved those more accustomed to a domesticated Spirit, consigned to familiar ecclesial rhythms.

The agenda set by Chung's address needs to be engaged. She has dared to challenge the docile image of the Spirit, one whose primary function is to bring comfort and harmony. She has dared to relate the Spirit to all living creatures and all ways of faith. She has dared to sully the Spirit by linking divine presence to those whose lives have not seen success, have not evidenced what usually is perceived as spiritual power. She has dared to embody the Spirit in her dancing protest rather than to circumscribe her experience of Spirit within texts that few outside the academic guild will read. How can we respond to her indictment, her well-posed challenge?

The purpose of this book is to reconfigure the sphere and character of the Spirit's action in order to provide a more holistic pneumatology. Relegated to matters of soteriological and ecclesiological efficacy in too many theological writings, the Spirit's movement and transforming work in all creation has been neglected. I will employ the winsome picture of the *perichoresis* in the life of God, expanding the metaphor to include creaturely life. This grounding image of the dancing, self-giving, outward flowing of the Trinitarian life of God invites the participation of all creation.

INVITING TO DANCE

The ancient idea of *perichoresis* will help us discover how the Spirit enables humans and all creation to participate in the life of God. The image was first proposed by creative theologians of the fourth century, the Cappadocians,[27] and treated more expansively by John of Damascus in the eighth century.[28] Because of the Damascene's work, the concept achieved currency in both East and West, and it became a standard conceptual tool not only to speak of Trinitarian relationships, but also to guard against tritheism and subordinationism.[29] *Perichoresis* depicts a relationship of mutuality in which persons draw their identity from being related to others. It is an ecstatic dance in which the Trinitarian persons literally "stand outside themselves" as they evoke the life of their divine counterparts.[30] It is movement, an interplay of self-giving that calls forth reciprocal sharing of life. *Perichoresis* "grasps the circulatory character of the eternal divine life."[31] This delightful divine choreography, which calls forth and deepens relationship, has implications for our dynamic self-understanding in the community of creation.[32]

Can we expand the image so that there is room for humanity—even for the whole of creation—to join in this dance within God's own life? Catherine Mowry LaCugna, along with other theologians, wants to employ *perichoresis* so as to include human persons. She suggests that "'the divine dance' is indeed an apt image of persons in communion: not for an intradivine communion but for divine life as all creatures partake and literally exist in it....The one *perichoresis*, the one mystery of communion includes God and humanity as beloved partners in the dance."[33] What pneumatological construction makes it possible for all creation to be included as a great company, moving gracefully or falteringly to the music that God alone fully hears? A carefully nuanced understanding of *perichoresis* will clarify the relationship between eternal and created spirit, and will allow us to talk about the interanimation. Early conciliar formulations of doctrine can both instruct and caution us. In Christology, through a "two natures" approach, too often the divine and human natures came across as oppositional constructs, displacing one another in various ways.[34] Language of Spirit, often absent in these early discussions, was what finally brought the hypostatic union into focus and clarity. A revitalized language of Spirit will help us see a world that can be understood relationally on all its levels.

Perichoresis originally was used by Gregory of Nyssa to speak of the mutual permeation of the Father[35] and the Son as an argument against the Arian denial of divinity to Jesus.[36] It did not take long to show its flexibility. Athanasius perceptively proposed that divinity could be communicated; it could move outside itself, even indwell that which is other without thereby being diminished.[37] In the subsequent fourth-century controversy about the nature and identity of the Spirit, the same notion of mutual coinherence between Christ and the Spirit allowed the church to affirm the Spirit as fully personal and fully divine.[38]

The development of the doctrine of the Trinity depended upon these prior affirmations and became the locus of much speculative theology about God's eternal life, unrelated to creation or humanity. LaCugna has carefully described the damage this has done; indeed, she argues that the preoccupation with the relations within God resulted in a "defeat of the doctrine."[39] If the doctrine of the Trinity is truly the story of God's outward movement to include, then *perichoresis* describes more than intratrinitarian relationships.

In the early church, the constructive delineation of God as Trinity presupposed the doctrine of the incarnation; Trinity was never about self-contained divine life. Had there been no encounter with the very life of God poured out through Jesus of Nazareth, the question of how this "Son of Humanity" relates to the eternal life of God would not have arisen. Then the throbbing awareness of presence after the departure of the Christ forced the fledgling church to articulate its threefold experience of God. The conclusion was radical and difficult to express: humanity is necessary to the unfolding of the divine life. Of course, this is only because God has willed it to be so; nevertheless, such an affirmation renders moot the propriety of tired debates about whether or not the human can be a "fitting vehicle to bear the divine." The affirmation speaks of the dignity of humanity, but even more of the humility of God. Only in the framework of a Trinitarian pneumatology can the tension be maintained.

Constructive theology has resisted intertwining divine being with human being in this intimate fashion. John Navone says it plainly: "We are not by nature participants in the divine nature or in the inner life of God."[40] He probably intends to safeguard the ontological difference between divine and creaturely being, but the tone of his statement diminishes the intrinsic relatedness to God inscribed by the creative working of the Spirit of God. His statement also reinforces, by what it leaves out, the idea that humanity alone relates to God. This focus on the personal, the "I-Thou" construct, recently has been challenged as an inadequate approach to the multiplicity of interactions that comprise a pneumatic worldview.[41] God relates to all that is, and in the Spirit all can participate in the movement of God. My goal is to provide a new vision of the interface between the life of God and created life. It is my belief that the Spirit makes mutual participation possible.

LEARNING THE STEPS

An expanded notion of *perichoresis* gives us a way to talk about the spiritual nexus that relates all creation to the Trinitarian history without succumbing to pantheism or to the hierarchical dualism that sharply separates the divine from the creaturely. It also provides a framework for a pneumatology that gathers up all created reality in the divine dance.

I am not alone in choosing to use *perichoresis* in contemporary constructive theology. Patricia Wilson-Kastner argues that the concept helps us see the shared life of God afresh, free of the patriarchal baggage that distorts the mutuality and liberty within the life of God and with all creation. She writes, "The divine trinitarian dance is a far more appealing, inclusive, and revealing sign of the divine than the two seated white males and a dove."[42] Furthermore, she employs *perichoresis* to describe a nonhierarchical, relational community, a human imaging of the divine life. Colin Gunton proposes the concept as theological grounding for the universal and particular. As the Trinitarian being of God celebrates both uniqueness and commonality, so should the human community prize distinctiveness as an ingredient in concern for the common good.[43] He goes further than does Wilson-Kastner by using the perichoretic analogy to speak of the relationality of all things, but does not evince the kind of ecological concern I would hope for. More concerned about the *aporias* of culture, he seeks to anchor historical and personal meaning in the transcendental reality of God, who cannot be subsumed.

Several streams flow into my work: the biblical witness,[44] classic formulations of the Spirit in historical theology, systematic attempts to configure the identity of the Spirit within the Trinitarian being of God, and the probings of selected contemporary theologians. In addition, I presuppose field theory drawn from modern physics, albeit here in simple, nonspecialist terminology, as it provides a creative way to describe the dynamic work of the Spirit in creation.[45] The Spirit is the force field where God's work is accomplished. Physicists since the groundbreaking work of Michael Faraday in the nineteenth century have spoken the language of *perichoresis* in describing the interrelatedness of the whole universe. I am claiming nothing less than this: *perichoresis* is an apt metaphor for the unfolding of the universe in the providence of God. Indeed, because *perichoresis* derives from reflection on God's involvement in space and time, it is "not conceptually foreign to createdness."[46]

It is commonplace in contemporary cosmological thinking to stress the interdependence of the whole universe, but many persons of faith wonder whether they should locate God within this matrix. Obviously, the creative "Let there be" demands that God be prior to creation; however, it is not possible to conceive of God apart from creation, even if we affirm the classic view of creation *ex nihilo*. God does not dwell in a parallel universe, separate from this spatiotemporal realm; hence, we must conceive of the God-world relationship as an organic whole without collapsing transcendence. An apt biblical way to speak of this relation is to use the concept of *kenosis*, a sharing of power through pouring it out on behalf of other agents.[47]

There are parallels between a perichoretic intuition and the conceptual framework of process theology. Filled with unique words and loaded with provocative concepts, process theology has concepts, offered by Whitehead and his followers, that are useful for a constructive pneumatology.[48] I appropriate images, borrowing from the pictures of the God-world relationship found in process theology, in order to draw out the implications of God's relatedness to time and space. Another fecund source of parallels is the Jewish mystical tradition known as Kabbalism.

My goal is to find a way to speak of the pervasive presence of God as Spirit that reflects biblical patterns and historic spiritual wisdom and responds to new thinking about power and movement in our evolving world. It will not do either to identify God with creation, or to abstract the divine from creation, leaving a purely naturalistic system. Monism and dualism are equally suspect, for both ignore the vitality of relationship.

Here are six primary theological presuppositions that shape this pneumatology:

1. God is inextricably related to the world. God is in the world, and the world is in God. This vision of panentheism—no bifurcation between God and the world—suggests a highly interactive

11

relationship. Transcendence and immanence are not descriptions of either-or, but of relatedness and movement. The God who cannot be contained suffuses all that is with holy presence, yet allows room for the flourishing of otherness. Perhaps most promising for constructive pneumatology is this insight of process theology, a model that ensures that God's immanence makes God neither identical with the world's creative processes nor absent from any of them. It also gives another way to think of the interface between the immanent and economic Trinity.

2. God gives the world creative space in which to flourish. Isaac Luria, a visionary sixteenth-century teacher of Kabbalism, articulates a doctrine of *tzimtzum*, which describes the movement of God's self-withdrawal so that there might be room for creation. While this space for creation is within the being of God, it is space to which God returns in the act of creation and redemption.[49] The cosmic process is comprised of these two movements: "Every new act of emanation and manifestation is preceded by one of concentration and retraction."[50] This voluntary self-limitation is at the same time an act of generous love. In kabbalistic tradition, the secret name for God is the "wide space," an image of spacious freedom for creation within the movement of God's ecstatic life. This vision is quite compatible with *perichoresis* and is a helpful way to describe the "field of the Spirit," a hospitable context in which newness is ever coming to be. Thus, a perichoretic pneumatology can articulate how all of creation participates in the life of God.

3. Many agents or factors are involved in the ongoing world process. Hence, traditional ways of speaking about God's power—ideas such as omnipotence or predestination—require critical examination. A coherent theology of the Spirit requires us to reconsider the nature of divine agency. In a world of process, where God freely shares power, rigid notions of sovereignty that ascribe all causality to the divine must be challenged.

Pneumatology offers a helpful paradigm of the mode of God's presence, an empowerment of all that is toward union with God.

4. Divine power is mediated and shared; there is openness to the future, the possibility of real novelty. Since God is not the all-determining power, we must construe divine action as "God-with." The work of the Spirit—hidden, nearly imperceptible, humble—is the paradigm of how God works in the world. "Force is no attribute of God," states the early Christian *Epistle to Diognetus*;[51] such insight challenges the view of God as dominative, always triumphing over all that opposes God's way. Many persons view the Spirit as the power that forcefully takes over one's personality. While there are biblical events and contemporary charismatic experiences that attest to this kind of action, we can rightly question if this is the normative way that the Spirit functions.

5. God as Trinity, eternally dwelling in self-giving relationship (*theologia*), chooses to include all creation in the *oikonomia* of creation and redemption. Yet it is not possible to consider these aspects of the divine life separately. All created things are contextualized in the movement of the divine life, from God's voluntary self-determination to create to the self-involving work of redemption. In this, I will be using Jürgen Moltmann's idea of the open, inviting Trinity. God's history with the world is Trinitarian, he believes, and this "triunity is open in such a way that the whole creation can be united with it and can be one within it."[52]

6. The Spirit is the point of contact between the life of God and the world that is yet coming to be. Described as "divine nearness,"[53] the Spirit makes possible the universal contact between God and history, between God and all creation.[54] Moltmann calls us to discover the "cosmic breadth of the Divine Spirit."[55] We must no longer speak about the Spirit only in connection with faith, the Christian life, the church, prayer, and relationship within the triune God; we must speak also in our day of the Spirit in connection with the body and nature, with the evolutionary movement of creation and transformation through resurrection.

My task is to understand what makes it possible for us to participate in the life of God, the inviting dance that welcomes all. What is the role of the Spirit in this? Answering this requires that we move beyond traditional soteriological affirmations—that is, the grace we receive through Christ allows the Spirit to indwell us and transform us. We must explore the prior relationship that all creatures have with God by virtue of being creatures constituted by God's breath. Can we go further? Through using the perichoretic intuition, can we include all created reality? I believe that we can and must, as I will argue in the next chapter.

NOTES

1. *Luther's Works*, vol. 40, ed. Conrad Bergendoff (Philadelphia: Fortress, 1958), 83.

2. A few exceptions should be noted: Dale Moody, *Spirit of the Living God: The Biblical Concepts Interpreted in Context* (Philadelphia: Westminster, 1968); Frank Stagg, *The Holy Spirit Today* (Nashville: Broadman, 1973); Wayne E. Oates, *The Holy Spirit and Contemporary Man* (Grand Rapids: Baker, 1974); and, much more briefly, David Emmanuel Goatley, "The Improvisation of God: Toward an African American Pneumatology," Memphis *Theological Seminary Journal* 33, no. 1 (spring 1995): 3–13; cf. Watson E. Mills, ed., *Speaking in Tongues: Let's Talk about It* (Waco, Tex.: Word, 1973); Robert H. Culpepper, *Evaluating the Charismatic Movement* (Valley Forge, Pa.: Judson Press, 1977). Recently, two Baptist theologians, Stanley J. Grenz, *Theology for the Community of God* (Grand Rapids: Eerdmans, 2000), and James W. McClendon Jr., *Systematic Theology: Doctrine*, vol. 2 (Nashville: Abingdon, 1994), have made the Spirit integral to their projects.

3. "The Fifth Theological Oration: On the Holy Spirit," in *Nicene and Post-Nicene Fathers of the Christian Church*, second series, ed. Philip Schaff and Henry Wace (New York: Christian Literature Company, 1894), 318.

4. See, for example, the following recent works: Leonardo Boff, *Trinity and Society*, trans. Paul Burns (Maryknoll, N.Y.: Orbis, 1988); David S. Cunningham, *These Three Are One: The Practice of Trinitarian Theology* (Oxford: Blackwell, 1998); Colin E. Gunton, *The Promise of Trinitarian Theology* (Edinburgh: Clark, 1990); Elizabeth A. Johnson, *She Who Is: The*

Mystery of God in Feminist Theological Discourse (New York: Crossroad, 1992); Catherine Mowry LaCugna, *God for Us: The Trinity and Christian Life* (San Francisco: HarperCollins, 1991); Thomas Marsh, *The Triune God: A Biblical, Historical, and Theological Study* (Mystic, Conn.: Twenty-Third Publications, 1994); Jürgen Moltmann, *History and the Triune God: Contributions to Trinitarian Theology*, trans. John Bowden (New York: Crossroad, 1992); and Ted Peters, *GOD as Trinity: Relationality and Temporality in Divine Life* (Louisville: Westminster John Knox, 1993).

5. For a considered analysis of this necessity, see Kilian McDonnell, "A Trinitarian Theology of the Holy Spirit?" *Theological Studies* 46 (1985): 191–227.

6. Ibid., 191.

7. Even though Christological insight preceded pneumatological understanding in the course of the church councils, the Spirit has not been reduced to the bond between the First Person and the Second Person of the Trinity, as much Western theology, following Augustine, has averred. One result of this Eastern accent is a different view of salvation as divinization, a growing participation in the life of God.

8. Johnson, *She Who Is*, 130.

9. Peter Hodgson offers a perceptive analysis of the reasons for the neglect of the Spirit: "In Western theology and philosophy the very concept of 'spirit' has for the most part been fraught with difficulties, conveying something vapid and dualistic, implying a separation of and hierarchy between the mental and the physical, the soul and the body, the human and the natural, the male and the female, the holy and the profane. The hierarchy reflects a suspicion and fear of the suppressed poles: nature, the body, and the feminine. Spirit had to be detached from these and controlled by means such as spiritualism and institutionalism, that is, through esoteric practices and male-dominated ecclesiastical office. Subordination of the Spirit, marginalization of women, and exploitation of nature have gone hand in hand in the history of the church" (*Winds of the Spirit: A Constructive Christian Theology* [Louisville: Westminster John Knox, 1994], 276).

10. Two groundbreaking pneumatologies are Jürgen Moltmann, *The Spirit of Life: A Universal Affirmation*, trans. Margaret Kohl (Minneapolis: Fortress, 1992) and Michael Welker, *God the Spirit*, trans. John F. Hoffmeyer (Minneapolis: Fortress, 1994). It is questionable whether Hodgson's *Winds of the Spirit* should be identified in this company. Although he offers perceptive insight into the doctrine of the Spirit, describing God's presence in the world as Spirit, his text is a larger systematic project in theology.

11. The provocative address of Chung Hyun Kyung at the World Council of Churches in 1991 has sparked much debate and helped bring pneumatology more into focus theologically. The address is printed in Michael Kinnamon, ed.,

Signs of the Spirit: Official Report, Seventh Assembly (Geneva: World Council of Churches, 1991), 37–47. See also Elizabeth A. Johnson, *Women, Earth, and Creator Spirit* (Mahwah, N.J.: Paulist Press, 1993); Rebecca Button Prichard, *Sensing the Spirit: The Holy Spirit in Feminist Perspective* (St. Louis: Chalice Press, 1999).

12. I am borrowing this concept from Ellen Charry. In *By the Renewing of Your Minds: The Pastoral Function of Christian Doctrine* (New York: Oxford University Press, 1997), she posits that doctrine has a pastoral function—that is, theological recovery shapes practice for contemporary Christians. Christian teaching therefore is not an abstraction, but a formative enterprise.

13. Moltmann, *The Spirit of Life*, 1–2, 34–37.

14. *Filioque* literally means "and from the Son." This addition in the Latin version of the creed of 381 (Niceno-Constantinopolitan) seemed, to the East, to suggest that there was more than one source of divinity within the being of God—that is, that somehow the monarchy of the First Person was being compromised.

15. This initially was more of a liturgical innovation; the phrase was not universally adopted until the eleventh century in the West.

16. Moltmann writes, "The defence of the Filioque by theologians of the Western church, contrary to the denial of it by Eastern theologians, led to a one-sided trinitarian doctrine in the West, and hindered the development of a trinitarian pneumatology" (*The Trinity and the Kingdom: The Doctrine of God*, trans. Margaret Kohl [San Francisco: Harper & Row, 1981], 178).

17. George S. Hendry, *The Holy Spirit in Christian Theology* (London: SCM, 1957), 23.

18. Ibid., 41.

19. I am indebted to my former doctoral student Jeffrey D. Vickery for this description of Chung's stirring presentation. See his unpublished dissertation, "Light from the East: Asian Contributions to Contemporary North American Theology" (Louisville, K.Y.: The Southern Baptist Theological Seminary, 1996), 232–234.

20. Kinnamon, ed., *Signs of the Spirit*, xiii.

21. Chung Hyun Kyung, "Come, Holy Spirit—Break Down the Walls with Wisdom and Compassion," in *Feminist Theology in the Third World: A Reader*, ed. Ursula King (Maryknoll, N.Y.: Orbis, 1994), 392

22. Chung Hyun Kyung, "Welcome the Spirit, Hear Her Cries: The Holy Spirit, Creation, and the Culture of Life," *Christianity and Crisis* 51 (July 15, 1991): 220.

23. Ibid., 221.

24. John Deschner, "Legitimating, Limiting, Pluralism," *Christianity and Crisis* 51 (July 15, 1991): 230.

25. Leonid Kishkovsky, "Ecumenical Journey: Authentic Dialogue,"

Christianity and Crisis 51 (July 15, 1991): 228. Cf. Michael Kinnamon's description of the reactions to the address (*Signs of the Spirit*, 15).

26. Chung was directly challenging a tradition that seeks to preserve the distinctiveness of a Christian pneumatology. Consider, for example, this statement by George Hendry in *The Holy Spirit in Christian Theology*: "The witness of the New Testament to the gift of the Spirit is soteriological and eschatological in character; when the attempt is made to fit it into the framework of a conception that is cosmological and anthropological in character, it almost certainly loses something of its distinctiveness" (16).

27. LaCugna offers an incisive analysis of the contribution made by the Cappadocians in formulating a theology of divine relations using the idea of *perichoresis* to counter the Arian claim of the creatureliness of the Son. The liability of this move, in her judgment, is the separation of the inner life of God (*theologia*) from God's life with creation (*oikonomia*) (*God for Us*, 53–73).

28. Verna Harrison, "Perichoresis in the Greek Fathers," *St. Vladimir's Theological Quarterly* 35, no. 1 (1991): 53–65.

29. See the analysis of Yves Congar, *I Believe in the Holy Spirit*, vol. 3, trans. David Smith (New York: Crossroad, 1997), 36–40.

30. The root meaning of perichoresis is drawn from the verb *perichorein*. According to Liddell and Scott, *chorein* means "to make room for another,"and *peri* means "round about." See Henry Liddell and Robert Scott, *Greek-English Lexicon* (Oxford: Clarendon, 1980), 634–635, 891.

31. Moltmann, *Trinity and the Kingdom*, 174.

32. For an excellent historical summary of the doctrinal development of perichoresis, see Michael G. Lawler, "Perichoresis: New Theological Wine in an Old Theological Wineskin," *Horizons* 22, no. 1 (1995): 49–66.

33. LaCugna, *God for Us*, 274.

34. Early theologians also used *perichoresis* to describe the reciprocal inherence of the human and divine natures of Christ.

35. I use the traditional designation "Father" when citing texts written before the shift in linguistic conventions that has made us more sensitive to the issues of inclusive, nonpatriarchal language. Currently, theologians and liturgists are experimenting with many metaphors for the triune God. In my judgment, using the traditional designations is far less important than retaining a triune structure for divine being.

36. Noted by LaCugna, *God for Us*, 72.

37. See Arthur C. McGill's profound study in *Suffering: A Test of Theological Method* (Philadelphia: Westminster, 1968), 80.

38. J. Patout Burns and Gerald M. Fagin, *The Holy Spirit* (Wilmington, Del.: Michael Glazier, 1984), 230.

39. LaCugna, *God for Us*, 198.

40. John Navone, *Self-giving and Sharing: The Trinity and Human*

Fulfillment (Collegeville, Minn.: Liturgical Press, 1989), 1.

41. Welker, *God the Spirit*, 41.

42. Patricia Wilson-Kastner, *Faith, Feminism, and the Christ* (Philadelphia: Fortress, 1983), 127. Cf. her later contribution with Ruth C. Duck, *Praising God: The Trinity in Christian Worship* (Louisville: Westminster John Knox, 1999).

43. Colin E. Gunton, *The One, the Three and the Many: God, Creation and the Culture of Modernity* (Cambridge: Cambridge University Press, 1993), 152–154.

44. I employ the NRSV as my primary translation; on occasion I provide my own translation, especially when it makes the language for God more inclusive.

45. As suggested by T. F. Torrance, *Space, Time, and Resurrection* (Grand Rapids: Eerdmans, 1976). Wolfhart Pannenberg has been influential in his appropriation of field theory as a means of interpreting the work of the Spirit. See especially his *Systematic Theology*, vol. 2, trans. Geoffrey W. Bromiley (Grand Rapids: Eerdmans, 1991), 79–114.

46. Gunton, *The One*, 167.

47. John Polkinghorne suggests that divine action in the world always pre-supposes *kenosis* (*The Work of Love: Creation as Kenosis* [Grand Rapids: Eerdmans, 2001]).

48. I am aware of two attempts to develop a process pneumatology: the brief and now dated work by Norman Pittenger, *The Holy Spirit* (Philadelphia: United Church Press, 1974), and more recently the thoughtful text by Blair Reynolds, *Toward a Process Pneumatology* (London and Toronto: Associated University Presses, 1990).

49. I am drawing from the classic source by Gershom G. Scholem, *Major Trends in Jewish Mysticism*, rev. ed. (New York: Schocken, 1946), 260–261.

50. Ibid., 261.

51. Cited in McGill, *Suffering*, 82.

52. Moltmann, *Trinity and the Kingdom*, 96.

53. Kilian McDonnell, "The Determinative Doctrine of the Holy Spirit," *Theology Today* 39, no. 2 (July 1982): 149.

54. Ibid., 150. McDonnell writes, "If one loses sight of the relation of the Spirit to creation and to the whole cosmic dimension, then there is no recourse to the Spirit to explain the character and quality of created reality."

55. Moltmann, *The Spirit of Life*, 10.

CHAPTER 2

VIVIFYING ALL CREATION

Where can I go from your spirit?
—Psalm 139:7

When you send forth your spirit, they are created;
and you renew the face of the ground.
—Psalm 104:30

THE WORD *OMNIPRESENCE* IS FAMILIAR TO THOSE ACQUAINTED WITH
Christian tradition, and the idea that God is to be found everywhere is widely accepted. However, the way we often speak
about the Spirit seems to deny this reality. We locate the Spirit in
rather specific, at times restrictive, places. We find the Spirit overshadowing the mother of Jesus, warming the heart of the
Christian, stirring the water of baptism, hovering over the
eucharistic meal, filling the hands of the ordained, or equipping
the body of Christ for ministry. Each of these locations relates to
the story of God's salvation through Christ and the church, and
certainly we are right to accent them—but not at the expense of
Scripture's clear refrain of the vivifying work of the Spirit in all
creation. Calling creation to lyrical life, the Spirit beckons all to
participate in the perichoresis of God with creation.

The omnipresence of the Spirit of God is a biblical assumption,
with significant implications for the life of God in creation. The
psalmist confesses that it is impossible to flee from God's Spirit
(Psalm 139:7); attempts to evade the divine presence are futile.
God finds even the one who "makes a bed in Sheol"—the last
place one would expect to encounter God. Ironically, even the

attempt to flee is sustained by the power and breath of God. God's universal presence as Spirit means that no realm, no creaturely being, is distant from the life of God; indeed, all things are located within God. This means that the Spirit, as the point of contact between God and the world, cannot be confined to the *ordo salutis*, the normative sequential order of salvation.[1]

This chapter reconsiders the sphere of the Spirit's movement, interfacing divine and human life, as well as the life of all creation. First, we will review the biblical and theological characterizations of the life-giving Spirit breathed into the world; second, we will reflect on the implications of this understanding toward a more ecologically focused theology; third, we will focus more particularly on the Spirit in human experience, a consideration more inclusive than the usual soteriological implications that we attach to the relationship of divine and human spirit. We must no longer speak about the Spirit only in connection with faith, the Christian life, the church, prayer, and spiritual formation; we must in our day speak also of the Spirit in connection with the body and nature, indeed of all created reality.

SHARING GOD'S BREATH

In this section I explore key terms used of the Spirit/spirit. It is neither an exhaustive analysis of the historical and literary contexts of the words nor an exegetical treatment, but a theological appropriation that will inform the constructive work of this text. The term *spirit* meant something very different to the people who wrote the Hebrew Scriptures from what it means to people today. When contemporary Christians hear the term *spirit*, they tend to set it in opposition to the term *matter*. We think of a spirit as something incorporeal, ethereal, and insubstantial. Not so for the biblical writers: Spirit was the powerful life force of God, and invariably it was to be encountered under the conditions of finitude.[2]

The pneumatological trajectory begins in Scripture[3] with the wind or Spirit of God hovering over the waters of chaos (Genesis 1:2). In contemporary versions of the Bible, the English word *spirit* translates the Hebrew word *ruach*, the predominant word used for both the divine and human spirit (e.g., Job 7:11; 27:3; Isaiah 63:14; 66:2). The ancient writers also use the term *ruach* to convey the idea of wind in motion (Genesis 8:1; Psalm 1:4) or breath (Genesis 6:3; 7:15). Breath meant life, and it is God who lends breath to all creatures, thus granting a share in God's Spirit. Conversely, idols have no breath, and consequently no spirit (Psalm 135:17; Habakkuk 2:19). Thus, they cannot rival God. Living people breathe; the dead breathe no more. Scripture stresses that the donation and withdrawal of breath discloses God's power over life and death. As Sallie McFague observes, "Our lives are enclosed by two breaths—our first when we emerge from our mother's womb and our last when we 'give up the ghost' (spirit)."[4] There is a mystery to life sustained by breath; when the biblical writers spoke of the *ruach*, or breath of God, they imagined a life force as powerful, uncanny, and uncontrollable as a desert sirocco.[5] They also stressed that spirit is not something that creatures "possess by permanent right,"[6] as Gary Badcock rightly argues.

Biblical characterizations of *ruach* are not always life-giving; the word sometimes carries sinister connotations. A blast from God's nostrils caused the sea to cover the Egyptians (Exodus 15:8,10)—the same *ruach* that had turned the sea into dry land (Exodus 14:21). God's anger can stir the wind to bring about cataclysmic weather to destroy idolatrous cultic places and practices (Ezekiel 13:13). At times, the *ruach Yahweh* seems to be destructive, but instead is restorative (Isaiah 30:28). God also can take breath or spirit away, which means the end of life in relationship (Psalm 51:11; 104:29). Because of the Spirit's close association with what could be perceived as natural processes, a great deal of ambiguity surrounds the Spirit's presence.

Creation theology in the Psalter sings of how all living things depend upon God for the breath of life: "By the word of [Yahweh] the heavens were made, and all their host by the breath of [God's] mouth" (Psalm 33:6). This creative work of the Spirit continually supplies presence and power: "When you send forth your spirit, they are created; and you renew the face of the ground" (Psalm 104:30). And all are enjoined to praise their maker and sustainer: "Let everything that breathes praise the LORD!" (Psalm 150:6). It is spirit, breath, that allows all to relate to God. The breath of life is God's vivifying presence; all who live do so by the power of spirit. God is the source of life not only in its beginning, but also in every breath that is drawn.

What closer intimacy can there be than shared breath? The portrait of God bending over lifeless clay to blow God's own breath into humanity, stirring creatures to life, conveys an intrinsic and tender relationship. Whereas theological tradition predominantly has used the concept of *imago Dei* to convey the correspondence between God and humanity, the biblical portrayal of *ruach* may surpass it in intimacy. Biblical writers do not seem to worry about the closeness between God and humanity that shared breath implies. For instance, Psalm 51:10-11 uses *ruach* in a twofold manner, referring to the Spirit of God and the spirit of the human: "Create in me a clean heart, O God, and renew a steadfast spirit within me. Do not cast me away from your presence, and do not take your Holy Spirit from me." Alasdair Heron notes how the "two senses are so intimately bound up together" that the word "becomes a linking term which refers both to God and to human life in its dependence upon God."[7]

Pneuma, the predominant Greek translation of *ruach*, carries a similar idea. God has granted breath to all creatures for the purpose of relationship with God.[8] Colin Gunton rightly contends that spirit is the medium of all relating: "That which is or has spirit is able to be open to that which is other than itself, to move

22

dynamically into relation with the other. Spirit enables a form of perichoresis to take place, between mind and world, world and God."[9] To speak of the Spirit as the medium of relating retains the ontological distinction between God and creatures.

Recently, theologians have returned to the primordial concept of the *ruach* in writing about the Spirit. Their efforts demonstrate the richness of this language for God. Donald Gelpi prefers to speak of the Spirit as the "Holy Breath." Applying this description to God and using varied imagery, he sees the *ruach* as the "transcendent, divine life force which nevertheless enters human experience as a source of gracious illumination....Far from being remote, abstract, or ethereal, the divine *ruach* enters human experience as an empowering enlightenment, as force for doing work."[10] Divine power or spirit does not displace human power or spirit; rather, it is the breath that blows through all creaturely life. The prevenient working of God's Spirit inspires the dance of all creation within the moving *ruach* of God.

Jürgen Moltmann offers a sustained reflection on the significance of *ruach* as a constructive way to illumine the scope of the Spirit's work in its cosmic context. Following Kraus's translation, he interprets *ruach* as "the confronting event of God's efficacious presence 'which reaches into the depths of human existence.'"[11] Yet Moltmann will not confine this description of God's presence to its indwelling of humans; indeed, it is the creative power of God in all created beings. Consistently he contends that the "possibility of perceiving God in all things, and all things in God, is grounded theologically on an understanding of the Spirit of God as the power of creation and the wellspring of life."[12] Similarly, McFague argues that following this trajectory in speaking of Spirit "suggests another possibility: that God is not primarily the orderer and controller of the universe but its source and empowerment, the breath that enlivens and energizes it.[13] She urges speaking of divine agency in terms of Spirit because it "undercuts anthropocentricism and promotes cosmocentricism."14

Another key term is *neshamah*, which also means breath. Writers tend to use it in a more comprehensive way than *ruach* in the Hebrew Scriptures to express the vivification of all creaturely life.15 The paradise story attributes the living vitality of all creatures (including humans) to the *neshamah* of God. It speaks of life constructed from "the unity of dust and breath,"16 as in Genesis 2:7. A closely related term is *nephesh*, which can be translated as "breathing creature." The Yahwist account in Genesis 2:19 narrates, So out of the ground the LORD God formed every beast of the field and every bird of the air, and brought them to the earth creature to see what this one would call them; and whatever the earth creature called every living soul [*nephesh hayyah*], that was its name.17

Qoheleth, the teacher-sage, links humanity and all creatures inextricably, as they share the same breath and spirit: "For the fate of humans and the fate of animals is the same; as one dies, so dies the other. They all have the same breath [*ruach*], and humans have no advantage over the animals; for all is vanity. All go to one place; all are from the dust, and all turn to dust again. Who knows whether the human spirit [*ruach*] goes upward and the spirit [*ruach*] of animals goes downward to the earth?" (Ecclesiastes 3:19-21; cf. 12:7). Although we may choose not to make focal the theological insights of this gloomy writer, the close kinship and destiny of all creatures is noted, which is an important affirmation as we trace the biblical terminology.

How should we regard the significance of the breath of God indwelling all creation? Many have feared to speak of divine presence in this way because they desire to preserve a greater ontological distinction between the Creator and the creaturely or the created. To speak of shared breath seems to blur this distinction, and it also displaces humans from their claim to be the only recipients of spirit. The throbbing vitality of God's own shared life as that which vivifies all creation seems to verge on animism or pantheism. If all draw breath given by God, do not all to some extent participate in divinity? Yes, if we mean that all nonhuman reality moves toward the end for which God purposes; yes, if we mean that all that live are within the "force field of the Spirit";[18] yes, if we mean that the open Trinity creates space for creatures to receive and compose life. We can say all of this without recourse to "spark of divinity" language.[19] God was meant to be our very breath. "We were to be healthy and full of life by breathing in the loving power,"[20] indeed the very presence, of God.

Yet this language of vivification is troubling. If the Spirit of life indwells all that is, how can we speak of the personal presence of God?[21] And how can we retain the identification of the Spirit as the Third Person of the Trinity? Perhaps we have difficulty speaking of the personal identity of the Spirit because of the hidden and humble patterns of the Spirit, the abiding aspect of God, who chooses to give life to others, thereby concealing divine identity through the enhancement of the personal in both God and humanity. (We will take up this idea in later chapters.)

At this point, it is important to stress that the Spirit of God and the spirit of humanity (and other creatures) are not identical, but are undeniably related. The Spirit of God evokes the spirits of all that are created, enabling them to participate in the perichoretic movement of God with creation, the dance of the universe. Gunton makes a helpful distinction when he suggests that whereas God is spirit, creaturely beings have spirit.[22] This stresses the ontological priority of God, who lends spirit in creation. All spirit is the gift of God; all spirit is sustained by the vivifying present of God's own spirit.

The Bible presents us with this problem by holding different descriptions of Spirit/spirit in tension. As we move further in the study, we will encounter other terms that challenge the ephemeral images of wind and breath. I believe that the emergent understanding of Spirit in Scripture and theology will allow us to affirm Spirit as both the vital power that pervades all creation and as the eternal Thou, relating to us at our most personal.

CARING FOR CREATION

Renewed interest in the well-being of creation can take several different approaches. I want to distinguish my construction of a pneumatic, perichoretic creation from what presently is known as "creation spirituality." Popularized by Matthew Fox, a former Roman Catholic priest, creation spirituality has provided a helpful corrective to a Western Christianity weighted toward a focus on redemption rather than creation.[23] The main concern of this approach is cosmological health; thus, Fox and others[24] challenge the streams within Christian tradition that they believe contribute to a negligible regard of this world. Rather than viewing salvation as otherworldly—something that removes us from this vale of tears—they celebrate the glory of creation as the joyous habitation of God's creatures. Creation spirituality also critiques Christianity's preoccupation with human beings and urges a much more inclusive and holistic theological concern that sees humanity as part of creation. These are strong contributions that have attracted many adherents. I am uncomfortable, however, with the unmitigated enthusiasm of these writers for this present world, which seems to ignore the grinding evolutionary pain born out of randomness. A romantic view of nature colors their perception—more utopian than realistic.[25] They also tend to blur creation and Creator as they attribute a level of sacredness to nature. Furthermore, they do not sufficiently address the unjust usage of the world's resources by those being encouraged to "celebrate the cosmos." In what seems to be a naïve perspective, they believe that if persons would see creation through the theological lens of creation spirituality, then they would gladly take up the requisite ecological advocacy.[26] Sin and oppression—what usually tempers such optimism—are marginal concerns.[27]

I also want to distinguish my approach from natural theology, the presumption that we can gain clear knowledge of God by observing the world. While the aim of natural theology—to speak in a credible way about God from experience in this world—is laudable, contemporary theologians have come to suspect its lofty claims. When I use the term "pneumatic creation," I am not trying to deify creation in the fashion of Spinoza, nor am I employing a theological methodology that finds proof of God's existence through the vestiges or traces of God found in creation.[28] Rather, I am speaking of creation as the context of shared life, divine and creaturely. God breathes Spirit into all that lives; the creation is the context for God and all created things to experience lively interdependence in the fashioning of a shared home.

Moving toward a more holistic pneumatology in which we view the world as God's body[29] could prompt new urgency in our collaborative responsibility for earth's healing.[30] The answer to the question "Who is my neighbor?" is expanded considerably by reflection on the cosmic breadth of the Spirit's presence. Unfortunately, Christian theology's preoccupation with humanity, its privileging of spirit over body and earth, and its apocalyptic eschatology with fiery scenes of earth's destruction have contributed to a trifling concern about God's will being done on earth. Sadly, those who serve in public office have far more to say about stewardship of natural resources (although their pronouncements are hardly sufficient) than we offer through the preaching and teaching in our churches.

The largest threat to the continuation of life on our planet is no longer nuclear warfare. As Michael Welker reminds us, the "worst way in which human beings are endangering themselves [and all other living creatures] is the erosion...of their biological-natural environments."[31] We are suffocating in our ever higher pile of garbage; living creatures are forced from plains and wetlands so that we might "develop" the area; we use resources with profligacy; species are becoming extinct, not through the grinding process of cosmic evolution, but through human violence. All creation is groaning; its subjection is far beyond what God intended when it was "subjected in hope," as Romans 8:20 puts it.

Indeed, it is only by the Spirit's enlivening that we can see the interdependency of all things—including God. As Catherine Mowry LaCugna contends, not only are we are constituted by our relationship to God, but also God is constituted by relating to us.[32] What, then, do our life-denying practices mean for the life of God? If the world is the realm of God's self-manifestation, then by our resistance to Spirit are we pushing creation toward the cross of extinction by our immolating behaviors? Dare we think that our practices, by which we are choking ourselves, leave little breathing room for the Spirit?

Anne Primavesi characterizes human awakening to the plight of the living communities to which we belong as the work of the Spirit. "It animates the gift of perception within us, opening our eyes to how things really are. It gives us the gift of *epikeia*, the ability to respond with sensitivity to the presence and reality of other living beings, creating relationships and exchanging energy."[33] Surely this is what is needed: a conversion of heart that we might yet accept our original vocation as God's partners in the care of this world.

Elizabeth Johnson writes lyrically of this powerful movement of Spirit (which she links closely to wisdom, Sophia) in and among human beings in taking up the work of forming and mending creation:

> She initiates novelty, instigates change, transforms what is dead into new stretches of life. Fertility is inti-

mately related to her recreative power, as is the attractiveness of sex....As mover and encourager of what tends toward stasis, Spirit-Sophia inspires human creativity and joy in the struggle. Wherever the gift of healing and liberation in however partial a manner reaches the winterized or damaged earth, or peoples crushed by war and injustice, or individual persons weary, harmed, sick, or lost on life's journey, there the new creation in the Spirit is happening.[34]

We live in a time of unprecedented natural cataclysms, many of our own making. What if we began to regard the world as the body of God? Would it make any difference in our practices if we perceived all creation as the embodiment of God? God is hungry in the streets of Somalia, where famine due to unsound ecological practices threatens the entire population. God is wheezing in the decimation of the rain forests, the lungs of the earth. God is bleeding in the packinghouses of North America where untold numbers of animals are slaughtered only to increase the obesity of their carnivores. God is drowning as global warming raises the sea level to overwhelm places of habitation. God's promise never again to destroy the world by flood is being vetoed by our love of engines, our refusal to live more simply.

The Spirit seeks to resuscitate the body of God by blowing through all creation with renewing, engendering power, yet cannot move through corridors blocked to her life-giving breath. Thus, we must become the Spirit's partners, caring for the pneumatic creation. Our insistent prayer and hopeful song must beckon God's work in a groaning creation.

Thus we sing: *Veni Creator Spiritus*, blow through our efforts your creative power; *Veni Creator Spiritus*, whistle through our care the joyous tune of your healing mercy; *Veni Creator Spiritus*, sing through all your creation the cadences of praise for the gift of shared life; *Veni Creator Spiritus*, pray through those with voices for those without voice to pray; *Veni Creator Spiritus*, embody the playful trust of providence for those too wounded to trust.

Thus we pray: Come, Holy Spirit, dear Comforter, and encourage and strengthen all of life. Vivify creation, that its groaning might issue in new life. Liberate creation from its sighs of desperation, its bondage to decay. Share your life-giving breath with all who move in concert with the life of God.

INSPIRITING ALL HUMANITY

The topic of spirituality has gathered much interest these days. Those books that have enjoyed a sustained tour on the *New York Times* best-seller list over the past few years include a generous sprinkling of ones on spirituality.[35] In this burgeoning market, one can find everything from *God's Daughters: Evangelical Women and the Power of Submission* (which I won't have time to read!), to *The Art Lover's Illustrated Guide to Spiritual Nudes* (which the aesthetically inclined have already read!), to the *Baptist Harley-Davidson Motorcycle Riders Devotional Bible* (actually, I fabricated this last one, but given the rest of the market, expect something like it).

And it is not just "religious folk" who use the term *spiritual*. Management techniques and leadership theory in corporate structures seek to infuse "spirituality" into their "mission statements." Even the former coach of the Chicago Bulls resorted to some notion of spirituality in order to transform unruly players who presented a significant challenge. "Spirituality" has become a booming industry that is avidly marketed alongside other "self-help" enterprises—kind of like dieting. Chant CDs, vision quests, pseudo–Native American rituals, corporate mission statements, and on and on—all point toward a deep spiritual hunger permeating American culture. Obviously, all that claims the word *spir-*

itual cannot pass for Christian spirituality. Indeed, the words of Diogenes Allen ring true: "One of the attractions of New Age spirituality is its vagueness about what is true outside one's own self."[36] Yet, rather than be snooty about our theological sophistication, we need to listen to this deep interest in the spiritual as telling us something important about the universal spirit, beckoning all to fullness of life. As Moltmann observes, "Because God's Spirit is present in human beings, the human spirit is self-transcendently aligned towards God."[37]

Are all persons "spiritual"? Indeed they are, by the power of God that sustains their lives. As we have seen, the fact that God shares breath with humanity allows a participation in the life of God at the most basic level. Johnson describes this intimate participation with Spirit as "the breath which a living person draws in and expels, as well as that utterly personal life force unique to each person that anchors identity at the same time that it gives aliveness and energy."[38] The Spirit gives us our personhood, fits us to encounter otherness, especially the otherness of God. Thus all persons are created to encounter God; human spirituality is because of the inspiriting action of God calling forth a creation that can hear and respond to God's address.

Because the spirit of the human is aligned toward God, every "true experience of the self becomes also an experience of the divine spirit of life in the human being. Every lived moment can be lived in the inconceivable closeness of God in the Spirit."[39] Hence we should no longer follow the triumphalist tradition in Christianity, which severely restricts the work of the Spirit to the baptized or ecclesiastical structures. Moltmann puts it forthrightly: "Men and women are not being taken seriously as independent people if they are only supposed to be 'in the Spirit' when they are recipients of the church's ministerial acts and its proclamation."[40] Furthermore, he urges, we must overcome "the false alternative between divine revelation and human experience of the Holy Spirit."[41] He is suggesting that we take the depth of human experience seriously, for it is an inchoate longing for the transcendent, the holy, the enduring.

We can also describe spirituality in terms of the divine inspiration that makes possible meaningful human living. God inspires (breathes into) the varied pursuits of humanity: teaching, dancing, writing, farming, governing, painting, plumbing, marrying, childrearing, singing, and so forth. Describing these phenomena inspired by the Spirit, Wolfhart Pannenberg writes, "They exhibit a particularly intensified life and are therefore attributed to an exceptional share in the life-giving spirit."[42] In a similar vein, Patrick Sherry believes that the inspiration of the Spirit "brings an enlargement of people's emotional and affective range, so that they can see and respond in new ways and thus 'surpass themselves' in their creations."[43] Perhaps it is too much to claim that all "inspired" persons would credit their contributions to the presence of God's Spirit; however, many know a measure of humility in recognizing power that comes from beyond them.

How can we encourage the genuine quest for God that opens humans out beyond themselves? As Pannenberg has pointed out, the measure of personhood in the divine life is not self-sufficiency, but precisely orientation to the other.[44] It seems wise for us to learn to welcome this sense of need, both in others and in ourselves. We humans try to satisfy our deep needs with superficial remedies; we must learn to value longing as telling us something about our deeper capacity. Arthur McGill, in his remarkable little book *Suffering* (required reading for my theology students until it went out of print), urges humans to learn to "rest in their need."[45] He writes, "Without need there would be no creative and fruit-bearing love in the world."[46] McGill was not reminding us of our deficiency; rather, he was articulating the central insight that we long for what only God can provide.

The spirituality of all humanity, a deeper awareness of longing than the rest of creation experiences (see Romans 8:19-25), prompts the human vocation of seeking God. This is the brooding, engendering work of the Spirit. Why should we affirm this of humans? St. Thomas takes as his own Plato's statement: "The individual nature of a thing consists in the way it participates in the perfections of God."[47] Humanity within creation is given the capacity to reflect God's beauty and goodness in that we are created to become "participants of the divine nature" (2 Peter 1:4). Yet other members of creation often display more clearly the glory of God, unhampered by the overt rebellion of humanity. All living things bear witness to the creative work of God in creation; in that, we cannot be isolated from creation, and should allow it to be our teacher as we "consider the lilies" (Matthew 6:28; Luke 12:27).

The Spirit of God can fruitfully be linked to beauty "as a reflection of divine glory, and a sign of the way in which the Spirit is perfecting creation."[48] The source of inspiration for beauty created by artists is the same as for beauty in the earth created by God: the breath that is Spirit.[49]

Many questions remain unanswered by this examination of the Spirit's vivifying work. We must ask: Is the Spirit's presence everywhere the same? How do human attitudes of receptivity or resistance affect the movement of God in creation as Spirit (recall the elder son who hears the sound of music and dancing but refuses to join in, thereby diminishing his own life as well as those of others [Luke 15:25-30])? Are there media for the Spirit's work that are more focused than sharing breath? How does the Spirit prompt recognition of the presence of God?

The work of the Spirit—hidden, nearly imperceptible, humble, often mistaken for something else—is the paradigm of how God works in the world. In the next chapter we explore the self-revealing of God in the gathering of a people.

NOTES

1. John McIntyre offers this reason for why the Holy Spirit has not been connected more with nature: "the close connection between the Holy Spirit and Christ, which has long been a feature of the doctrine of the Holy Spirit and which on the whole has tended to tie the Holy Spirit to the *opus ad extra* of fulfilling the purpose of salvation in human terms, and not also in terms of the rest of the created order" (*The Shape of Pneumatology: Studies in the Doctrine of the Holy Spirit* [Edinburgh: Clark, 1997], 192).

2. This theme is constantly stressed by Michael Welker, *God the Spirit*, trans. John F. Hoffmeyer (Minneapolis: Fortress, 1994).

3. I will follow neither a strict literary sequence nor historical sequence in my treatment of representative biblical texts, although I will at times distinguish between early perspectives and later developments.

4. Sallie McFague, *The Body of God: An Ecological Theology* (Minneapolis: Fortress, 1993), 143.

5. Michael E. Lodahl contends that the biblical writers seek to "tame" the mysterious and unpredictable functioning of the Spirit, trying to make the activity of God as Spirit more comprehensible (*Shekinah/Spirit: Divine Presence in Jewish and Christian Religion* [New York: Paulist Press, 1992], 46–47).

6. Gary D. Badcock, *Light of Truth and Fire of Love: A Theology of the Holy Spirit* (Grand Rapids: Eerdmans, 1997), 9.

7. Alasdair I. C. Heron, *The Holy Spirit* (Philadelphia: Westminster, 1983), 7.

8. Acts 17:25-27 employs a cognate of *pneuma* to describe the gift of breath from God to all living.

9. Colin E. Gunton, *The One, The Three and The Many: God, Creation and the Culture of Modernity* (Cambridge: Cambridge University Press, 1993), 185.

10. Donald L. Gelpi, *The Divine Mother: A Trinitarian Theology of the Holy Spirit* (Lanham, Md.: University Press of America, 1984), 11. See also Gelpi, *The Spirit in the World* (Wilmington, Del.: Michael Glazier, 1988).

11. Jürgen Moltmann, *The Spirit of Life: A Universal Affirmation*, trans. Margaret Kohl (Minneapolis: Fortress, 1992), 42.

12. Ibid., 35. For a sustained reflection on the metaphor of God as wellspring, see David S. Cunningham, *These Three Are One: The Practice of Trinitarian Theology* (London: Blackwell, 1998).

13. McFague, *The Body of God*, 145.

14. Ibid., 144.

15. The flood story also describes "the breath of life" of all living things as that which gives them their historical existence (Genesis 7:22).

16. I am borrowing this phrase from my revered teacher Dale Moody. See his *Spirit of the Living God: The Biblical Concepts Interpreted in Context* (Philadelphia: Westminster, 1968), 11.

17. In using "earth creature," I am following Phyllis Trible, *God and the*

Rhetoric of Sexuality (Philadelphia: Fortress, 1978).

18. The terminology is that of Wolfhart Pannenberg, *Systematic Theology*, vol. 1, trans. Geoffrey W. Bromily (Grand Rapids: Eerdmans, 1991), 382–383. Pannenberg borrows from the field theory of quantum physics to interpret the Spirit of God in a scientifically cogent manner.

19. This Platonic language mars the otherwise helpful treatment of George A. Maloney, *The Spirit Broods Over the World* (New York: Alba House, 1993), 42.

20. Ibid., 38.

21. According to McFague, "One of the great assets of the model [of the Spirit as the source and renewer of life] is precisely its amorphous character in contrast to the highly human, personal, and androcentric nature of Father and Son: spirit is not necessarily human, personal (though it is relational), or male. In fact, it is often has been designated female; but it may be best that, for once in Christian reflection, we let God be 'it'" (*The Body of God*, 147).

22. Gunton, *The One*, 188.

23. Fox's major works are *Original Blessing: A Primer in Creation Spirituality* (Sante Fe, N. Mex.: Bear, 1983); *The Coming of the Cosmic Christ: The Healing of Mother Earth and the Birth of a Global Renaissance* (San Francisco: Harper & Row, 1988); and *Creation Spirituality: Liberating Gifts for the Peoples of the Earth* (San Francisco: HarperSanFrancisco, 1991).

24. Thomas Berry is also a significant figure in this contemporary movement. His writings include *The Dream of the Earth* (San Francisco: Sierra Club Books, 1988), and, with Thomas Clarke, *Befriending the Earth: A Theology of Reconciliation Between Humans and the Earth* (Mystic, Conn.: Twenty-Third Publications, 1991). In some ways, Berry is the intellectual heir to the work of Teilhard de Chardin.

25. McFague, *The Body of God*, 72.

26. Fox, *Creation Spirituality*, 29.

27. In fairness to Fox, he has written on sin in a recent book, *Sins of the Spirit, Blessings of the Flesh: Transforming Evil in Soul and Society* (New York: Three Rivers Press, 1999), albeit without the traditional Augustinian trappings that he so vigorously challenges in *Original Blessing*.

28. For a nuanced analysis of the *vestigia* tradition in theology, see Cunningham, *These Three Are One*, 89–119.

29. I am indebted to McFague for this concept. She has constructed her holistic pneumatology using the metaphor of the world as "God's body," a considerable expansion of St. Irenaeus's portrayal of the Spirit as the "soul of the church."

30. Rather shocking is Rosemary Radford Ruether's *Gaia and God: An Ecofeminist Theology of Earth Healing* (San Francisco: HarperSanFrancisco, 1992), which is written with minimal reference to the Spirit, although with

vague reference to "spirituality."

31. Welker, *God the Spirit*, 303.

32. The sustained argument of her *God for Us: The Trinity and Christian Life* (New York: HarperCollins, 1991) is grounded in the suffering, indwelling, communal relationship that God shares with humanity.

33. Anne Primavesi, *From Apocalypse to Genesis: Ecology, Feminism and Christianity* (Minneapolis: Fortress, 1991), 260.

34. Elizabeth A. Johnson, *She Who Is: The Mystery of God in Feminist Theological Discourse* (New York: Crossroad, 1992), 135.

35. *The Bowker Annual Library and Book Trade Almanac*, 41st ed., ed. Dave Bogart (New Providence, N.J.: R. R. Bowker, 1996), notes that books on spirituality "seem to be crossing over in the general-trade market" (615). The 1997 edition of the *Annual* assesses the place of books on religion among the bestsellers: "This year, religion and spiritual titles account for six of the top 30 nonfiction titles; in fiction, those categories accounted for five of the top 30" (594).

36. Diogenes Allen, *Spiritual Theology: The Theology of Yesterday for Spiritual Help Today* (Cambridge, Mass.: Cowley, 1997), 159.

37. Moltmann, *Spirit of Life*, 7.

38. Johnson, *She Who Is*, 131.

39. Moltmann, *Spirit of Life*, 35.

40. Ibid., 2.

41. Ibid., 5.

42. Wolfhart Pannenberg, "The Doctrine of the Spirit and the Task of a Theology of Nature," *Theology* 75, (January 1972): 8–21.

43. Patrick Sherry, *Spirit and Beauty: An Introduction to Theological Aesthetics* (Oxford: Clarendon, 1992), 88.

44. Pannenberg, *Systematic Theology*, vol. 1, 426–427, 430.

45. Arthur C. McGill, *Suffering: A Test of Theological Method* (Philadelphia: Westminster, 1968), ch. 6.

46. Ibid., 100.

47. Thomas Aquinas, *Summa Theologica* 1.14.6.

48. Sherry, *Spirit and Beauty*, 2.

49. Exodus 31:3 offers an example of this inspiration in Bezalel, of whom God says, "I have filled him with divine spirit, with ability, intelligence, and knowledge in every kind of craft."

CHAPTER 3

GATHERING A PEOPLE

I will put my spirit within you, and you shall live.
—Ezekiel 37:14

CROSSING BOUNDARIES, CONJURING RESISTANCE, AND CREATING alliances, the Spirit works to gather a people to be a particular expression of God's presence in the world. Charting the movement of the Spirit presents quite a challenge because of tensions in the different layers of Scripture and the varied theological interpretations. Yet by examining biblical materials and probing their theological insights, we can see an emerging gestalt that identifies divine presence in the world gathering a people. What appears is undoubtedly iconoclastic toward simplistic perspectives, for Spirit remains an elusive idea in describing the nature of God in relationship to humanity. Remarkably, the biblical view of Spirit gathering a people can best be understood as an empowerment of human participation.

Thus far we have explored the presence and function of the Spirit in a universal, creative sense. The Spirit is the divine presence vivifying all creation, supplying breath and power. Spirit sustains all that is, giving energy and guiding the movements of the dance of life. We should not assume, however, that when the ancient writers spoke of *ruach* they had a developed understanding of the Spirit of God, or Holy Spirit. They did not, although they had clear intuitions that the sustaining life force was not under human control, nor were the purposes of this mysterious presence within their grasp. Implicitly they understood that the transcending Spirit, none other than God, who beckoned them to response and relationship, enlivened the meaningful currents of their lives.

The narratives of Scripture move beyond an impersonal and generalized sense of Spirit and speak of the mission of the Spirit in gathering a people. The work of the Spirit is not disincarnate[1] in either Testament, although elemental forces such as fire and wind and water are also means of the Spirit's action. Clearly, there is development in the understanding of the biblical writers as they move from the enigma of early expressions of Spirit toward a more lucid articulation of the Spirit's relationship to messianic expectations. A tension between the one (a leader) and the many (a people) often ensues in the texts that seek to articulate an inchoate perception of God as Spirit, who is active in the formation of a community that would function as God's own.[2]

Critical questions press for engagement. Is the Spirit everywhere present in the same way? Can the workings of the Spirit be unmistakably perceived? Is the Spirit's activity always indubitably holy? Tracing the biblical witness of God's history with Israel and the church would suggest that the answer to these questions is no.

Furthermore, when we examine the stories of Scripture, we encounter unusual occurrences that challenge our present interpretive frameworks, characterized as they are by rationalism and psychological theory. How can we understand the idea of a Spirit taking over persons, causing them to act in a frenzied manner? Does this not suggest a violent and coercive manner at odds with the conventional biblical portrait of the gentle, indirect impress of the Spirit? Can an idea of genuine collaboration between God and humanity be sustained in the face of these figurations of unbridled power?

In this chapter I examine the Spirit's role in forging and sustaining community, a gathered people, within the historical compass of the Hebrew Scriptures. Later chapters will examine the community of the church and God's movement within and beyond it. Here we explore the movement of the Spirit indwelling leaders, forming community, instructing in word and wisdom, and promising a messiah.

INDWELLING LEADERS

Early attestations of the Spirit's work are fraught with ambiguity. Varied texts describe the work of the Spirit indwelling key figures, empowering them for feats of strength, leadership roles, prophetic proclamations, or representative functions in the cult. In each instance, the Spirit is utilizing an individual for corporate purposes—that is, gathering and forming an identifiable people as God's own. For some, this indwelling seems to be a long-term abiding; for others, the Spirit rushes upon them and then departs. What determines this is unclear. The Spirit seems to function with a radical freedom, choosing persons to be instruments of God without regard for usual standards of competence. Apparently, disobedience does not automatically disqualify one for this indwelling, as the Samson stories would suggest (Judges 14–16), and repentance does not ensure that God's Spirit will remain, as the saga of Saul inexorably recounts (1 Samuel 15:24-35).

We will consider these two figures briefly, as we find in them a primitive understanding of Spirit that stubbornly persists in later epochs. The narratives that chronicle their ventures show disparate editorial hands, thus we must pierce beneath the surface of these accounts to ascertain the developing traditions about the Spirit.

Samson is not a particularly attractive religious leader, given his varied self-aggrandizing pursuits and lack of discipline, yet the action of the Spirit in his life affords preservation of the people in a situation of affliction and fragmentation.[3] Delineating the experience of the power of the Spirit of God in Samson's life is thoroughly ambiguous, hence divergent interpretations and feelings abound—in his time and ours. George Montague notes that in these early episodes, "the motion by the spirit is direct upon the individual and not tied to any institution or rite,"[4] which may indicate the reason for their ambiguity.

Repeatedly, Judges 13–16 emphasizes that the Spirit of God fell upon Samson. In light of this, we are prompted to question whether the presence of the Spirit "seems to make possible nothing more than escape-artist stunts and tricks for conquering lions, brawling, and murdering."[5] Involved in all sorts of unsavory things, Samson nevertheless was "stirred" or "impelled" by the Spirit of God (Judges 13:25). The Spirit is implicated in it all, even in the final humiliation of a life that Samson could never devote fully to God.[6] Perceptively, Michael Welker writes, "The action of the Spirit is by no means necessarily connected with joy and good fortune for the person who bears the Spirit and for this person's surroundings!"[7] Certainly, this is true of Samson, and Welker's insight proves helpful as we challenge some of the domesticated ideas of the Spirit throughout this study. The Spirit does not overcome Samson's many failings—his swaggering provocations to the Philistines that tarnish his vocation as a Nazirite. Nevertheless, the Spirit makes possible the preservation of Israel through him. It would not be wise, however, to take this seemingly theologically bankrupt tale as paradigmatic of the ways of Spirit, especially in light of millions not preserved when faced with those bent on their destruction as a people.[8] Theological reservations notwithstanding, this primitive characterization of Spirit demonstrates that God chooses to be implicated in the machinations of sinful humans.

Saul is another tragic hero, marked out by the Spirit to do battle for the threatened tribes of Israel as they seek to sustain life amidst heightened challenges from the Philistines. For the first time, we see the Spirit connected to the anointing of a leader as Samuel commissions Saul "to govern the Lord's people Israel, and to save them from the grasp of their enemies round about"

(1 Samuel 10:1). The Spirit does not come upon Saul immediately, but Samuel prophesies that he will receive the spirit and "will be changed into another man" (1 Samuel 10:6) as Saul joins in the cultic activities of the band of prophets he will meet on his way to Gilgal. Caught up in a state of religious fervor, expressed through a cacophony of instruments and ecstatic speech, Saul has been seized by the Spirit, conscripted to serve the people through a power that makes him suspect. We learn of this suspicion by the cynical way others question his new status: "Is Saul also among the prophets?" (1 Samuel 10:11). A recurring theme in Scripture is the dubitable status that accompanies one who claims to serve "in the power of the Spirit."[9]

For the biblical scholar and the theologian, the most perplexing aspect of Saul's relation to spirit is the notice that after the Spirit of the Lord departed from him, he was tormented by an evil spirit sent by the Lord (1 Samuel 16:14). Explicitly, the writer speaks of the "evil spirit from God" no less than four times in this passage. What are we to make of the anointed leader of God being left to fend off the malevolent power (God?) without the Spirit of God? With little explanation, the ancient writer says that the reason for this is that God has rejected Saul as king because of his disobedience (see the account of this rejection in 1 Samuel 15). It is hard not to level the charge of favoritism at God, as a similar fate does not befall David, someone equally reprobate in moral concerns.[10] Here the radical freedom of the Spirit could not be more telling or disturbing. If the Spirit of God departs from a person, how is it possible to continue to live?

Moreover, how are we to interpret the notion of an evil spirit from God? This is not as rare an idea in the Hebrew Scriptures as we might think (cf. Judges 9:23; 1 Samuel 18:10; 1 Kings 22:21), although it is more characteristic of older strata.[11] The usual surmise of biblical scholars and theologians is that at this point in biblical theology there is not even the modified dualism that would allow a source other than God for a spirit, even a malign spirit. Some interpreters attempt a psychological analysis of this and similar episodes, perceiving the text to be about a troubled state of mind rather than a roaming "spirit."[12] Clearly, our questions run ahead of the theological sophistication of those narrating the early monarchical period of Israel's history. Their concern was more to buttress the idea that the sovereignty of God is demonstrated in withdrawing and sending S/spirit[13] as God determines. Further, the writings suggest that the spiritual nature of humans is not easily determined.

The depiction of Saul once again experiencing the prophetic frenzy, even after the rejection by God and the withdrawal of God's Spirit (1 Samuel 19:23), defies any systematic resolution. Has the Spirit of God returned once more, or is this a parody of charismatic indwelling? Saul's bizarre behavior suggests that identifying the presence of the spirit is difficult, that facile conclusions leave too many questions unanswered. In many respects, this dilemma continues in the New Testament and rears its head even today. How do we "define what authentic experience of the Spirit and authentic spirituality are?"[14] I will attempt to address this issue of discernment of "spirits" in chapter 7, where I take up the idea of "winnowing."

Other texts that deal with the work of the Spirit are easier to assay. As we survey the textual data of the activity of the Spirit, we are amazed by the stunning variety of activities credited to this indwelling. In the tumultuous life of Joseph, the Spirit is the source of extraordinary powers: interpretation of dreams, perceptive financial planning, wise administration, and the capacity to forgive his treacherous brothers (Genesis 41–43). In the lengthy epic of Moses, the empowering presence of God accompanies his sojourn from Egypt through wilderness toward the land of promise. Although an explicit identification of the Spirit is marginal to the thick Mosaic strands of Scripture, the figurations of divine presence are manifold in flame and water, miracle and provision. Most revelatory is the unreserved communication between God and Moses—a reciprocal movement of spirit.[15] Moses' challenge to the hegemony of Pharaoh over the lives of his Hebrew kinsfolk, competition with the magicians of the realm, and development of a strategy for liberation express indwelling power through the agency of this "meek" man.

Although subordinated in the heroic tale of her brother, Miriam also moves to the rhythm of the Spirit's indwelling.[16] Wise in her protection of her younger brother, she helps strategize his survival. Through subversive collusion with her mother, Miriam is a shrewd instrument of the Spirit's liberating project. The Scriptures ascribe to her the status of a prophet (Exodus 15:20), and although the patriarchal overtones of the Exodus narratives circumscribe her leadership more narrowly than that of her brothers, she often is mentioned with them as the ones chosen to lead Israel (e.g., Numbers 26:59; 1 Chronicles 6:3). What marks Miriam as one the Spirit indwells? Perseverance in the desert crossing, worship leadership (Exodus 15:21), the affirmation of the people regarding her significant role (Numbers 12:15), and her long shadow in the history of the Exodus (Micah 6:4) all attest to distinctive spiritual empowerment in her life.

Joshua, like his predecessor Moses, was perceived to be a charismatic leader, one "in whom is the spirit"(Numbers 27:18; cf. 11:17). The passages detailing the succession of leadership from Moses to Joshua do not use the language of Holy Spirit; however, God can transfer to the chosen successor that "spirit" which indwells Moses in his many exploits. This implies that it is divine presence working through the one whom God and Moses together had marked out for continuing leadership; "spirit," thus, is not to be equated with the personal giftedness of Moses, yet not unrelated to it. Likewise, God distributed some of the "spirit" of Moses to the elders commissioned to assist him in the arduous task of adjudicating the demands of a contentious people. We can see that the transmission of spirit is not the sole prerogative of the endowed leader.[17]

A similar account of the sharing of the charismatic spirit is found in the Elijah-Elisha cycle, particularly the departure scene (2 Kings 2:9,15). Elisha requests a "double portion" of his master's spirit. Miraculously his request is granted, because he sees Elijah taken up from the earth in a mysterious way. Montague cautions the reader of this text not to let questions about the fiery chariot and the heavenly whirlwind obscure the Deuteronomist's real concern.[18] The tradition portrayed the Spirit as the controlling power in the prophet's life, making him appear and disappear in a flurry of unpredictable sequences (e.g., 1 Kings 18:7-12), and so the climactic conclusion of his life should not surprise. The transmission of charismatic spirit from Elijah to Elisha is dependent upon seeing the wonder; that Elisha does see assures the reader that the spirit has come to rest upon Elisha, just as it had upon his spiritual father. Seeing is focal; thus, it is repeated three times in the pericope. The Spirit is the medium for discerning divine presence; Spirit is the matrix in which God's empowering occurs.

Another early strand of the Deuteronomist's history speaks of the result of the indwelling power of the Spirit, albeit more as an allusion than directly. A good example of this is the story of Deborah, a judge as well as a charismatic military leader of the people during the early settlement period; she also is described as a prophet (Judges 4:4). Certainly this must mean that she is inspired by the *ruach Yahweh*. The presence of God with her is palpable as she accompanies the dubious Barak into battle. Curiously echoing words of God to Moses, Barak says to Deborah, "If you will go with me, I will go; but if you will not go with me, I will not go" (Judges 4:8; cf. Exodus 33:15). Indeed, she symbolizes the very presence of God as she offers encouragement and assurance that her triumphant note of victory will be realized (Judges 4:14). In the story of Deborah we have a proleptic witness to the Spirit being poured out on all, women as well as men. Her witness to indwelling anticipates the insight of later prophets (e.g., Joel 2:28-29; Ezekiel 18:31).

The New Testament continues the idea of the Spirit indwelling specific leaders for ministry, though it is a more nuanced and inclusive treatment. Although biblical interpreters usually try to see the mystery of God's activity resolved in light of the story of Jesus, the role of Spirit retains some of the mystery of the movement of God in the world through God's people. We will take up these issues in a later chapter.

FORMING A COMMUNITY

The *missio Dei* (God's universal mission) as narrated in the historical and prophetic books of the Hebrew Scriptures is to form a community to share in this mission. The community of God's people will be characterized by the worship of Yahweh, distinctive ethical sensitivity to strangers and the oppressed, and an inclusive sense of mission that extends to the whole world.

Although thus far I have been focusing on individual leaders who were used by the Spirit in distinctive ways, I do not intend to abstract them from the community of which they were a part. Welker suggests that even the early experiences of God's Spirit by individuals are focused toward "restoring the community of God's people."[19] Recall Ezekiel's vision (Ezekiel 37:1-11); it is the Spirit who makes a community alive. The Spirit of the Lord carries the prophet into a valley of dry bones and demonstrates for him that without the *ruach* of God, no life remains, all are cut off from community and the presence of God. Yet the Spirit can restore life and vivify a people to serve God once again. In this profoundly corporate image of the reconstituting of the people of

45

God, the forming work of the Spirit is essential.

The Spirit also forms a community through worship. Scholars of liturgy observe that worship is profoundly formative in that it gives identity and draws individuals into a pattern of relationship larger than themselves.[20] The evocative breath of Spirit makes worship possible, as persons are addressed by the Holy One in their midst. Inspired to wonder, to longing, to praise, and to faith, the worship of the people of God is suffused with divine spiritual presence. Echoes of Israel's worship can be found in the Psalter, a fecund repository of canticle and prayer, memory and hope. Reverberating throughout the 150 psalms are the sounds of Spirit, who serves as cantor of song, prompter of prayer, breath for praise, and energy for dance.[21] The Spirit enlivens worship, moving it toward encounter with God.

Another way in which the Spirit is instrumental in forming community is as the power to cross barriers, to welcome those who are outsiders or of lesser status. Inscribed deeply in the legal code is an ethic of generous hospitality toward the "stranger" (Leviticus 19:33-34).[22] Israel's own history of being strangers in a foreign land (or actually being without permanent home for generations) was to stand as a reminder to practice ways of tangible inclusion—shelter, meals, an invitation to share in worship.

Over a period of fifteen hundred years, no matter where the Hebrews were located, their home life and especially their worship focused on the stranger. This meant not only welcoming itinerants, but also finding ways to care for widows and orphans in their midst and showing compassion for the poor. The prophets were implacable in rebuking Israel whenever they failed to reserve a place for the stranger or acted in an oppressive way toward those with marginal status (e.g., Isaiah 56:3; Jeremiah 22:3; Ezekiel 22:29). God's people, therefore, were to welcome others, remembering that they too had been strangers, aliens, in the land of Egypt. The Spirit's gathering and forming of community stretched the boundaries of inclusion.

Over and over we see persons of disparate backgrounds—Ruth the Moabite, Rahab the Canaanite, Naaman the Syrian—woven into the tapestry of the people of God. Supplied with spiritual strength, at times sufficiently subversive to transcend Israel's overly rigid boundaries, these figures make supple and rich the community formed by the power of God's presence. Belonging to the people of God surely was more than a matter of tribal or ethnic ancestry; it had to do with trust in God and willingness to join in the traditions of worship as Israel understood them, dancing with the cadences of Israel's faith. The Spirit-empowered crossing and blurring of boundaries reconfigures the identity of the community, which scandalizes those who believe in exclusive strictures for "belonging." The challenge of "exclusion or embrace" will be sharpened further as we explore this theme in the ministry of Jesus.[23]

God's mission to Israel carries import for the whole world. The midwifery of the Spirit in birthing a people was never for the benefit of Israel alone. Rather, the community drawn together in Spirit was to be a channel of gracious inclusion for all seekers of the true God. Provinciality and xenophobia, however, often eclipse the way of welcome and incorporation. Suspicion of the stranger often issues in violence. Where is the Spirit to be found in this?

It is customary to link the Spirit with gathering and renewing a people, not with the violence and wrath that readers of the Bible associate with a monarchical vision of God.[24] Yet the Spirit at times moves with fury against the enemies of God's people, those who would impede the work of gathering and forming a hospitable community. Judges contains several accounts of the Spirit coming upon various leaders to perform acts of vengeance in the name of Israel's God (Judges 3; 6–7; 11). Mark Wallace warns against construing a "theology that tries to sidestep these biblical witnesses to the Spirit's warrior identity," for it becomes "a theology that falsely projects a truncated portrait of the Spirit."[25] The task of rendering a synthesis of the visions of Spirit within the Hebrew Scriptures remains somewhat intractable, and we must keep Wallace's admonition in mind.

INSTRUCTING IN WORD AND WISDOM
Students of the Hebrew Scriptures have at times treated Spirit and Word as if they were competitive or mutually exclusive aspects of the divine revealing. This is due in part to the emerging patterns in the Hebrew Scriptures. Whereas earlier textual layers had spoken of the Spirit "coming upon" a particular figure to enable certain mighty works, later witnesses accent the prophetic word as the medium of the will and presence of God. For example, the story of the ministry of Huldah (2 Kings 22:14-20) does not mention the empowering presence of the Spirit of God; maybe it is assumed, but more likely the correlation between prophetic word and Spirit has become suspect at this time.

What does seem clear is that the later writing prophets disassociate themselves from the ecstatic prophets of earlier times.[26] Amos puts it bluntly: "I am no prophet, nor a prophet's son" (Amos 7:14). More pointed and problematic is the denunciation of Jeremiah: "The prophets are nothing but wind [*ruach*], for the word is not in them" (Jeremiah 5:13). Spirit and prophetic word are sundered in this text. A further development is the silencing of prophecy as the written word, Torah, moves to the place of privileged authority. Rather than viewing these expressions of revelation in a supersessionist manner, we should regard them as complementary media. Each is a means of the Spirit's instruction to receptive humanity. Spirit and Word must remain in a mutually interpretive relationship.

Similarly, Wisdom and Torah have been seen as unrelated or alternative means of mediating the divine presence. Wisdom theology, because it is more experientially grounded in the observation of creation, rarely has been accorded the status of Torah theology, which is drawn from the literature more grounded in historical deeds.[27] Word has been associated with Torah and prophecy; Wisdom has been associated with the traditions of the sages.

Some scholars warn against thinking of Word or Spirit or Wisdom as intermediary beings between God and the creation. Rather, they are simply distinctive ways of referring to God's active presence.[28] We should heed this caution. While each of these characterizations of God speaks of the diverse ways that God can dynamically communicate purpose and personal relation with the creation, all can be understood as the confronting presence of the One we can know only in Spirit, who mediates both Word and Wisdom.

Wisdom often is the form in which God approaches humans— as angry prophet (Proverbs 1:20-33), as agent of creation, as one who speaks as only God can speak: "Whoever finds me finds life" (Proverbs 8:35). The female figure of Wisdom has drawn much attention in recent years.[29] This is partly because feminist biblical scholarship is burgeoning, and many are addressing this long-neglected area. In addition, those concerned with crafting inclusive liturgies have found a fecund source in the Sophia (*hokmah*) language of the Bible. Perhaps this appropriation is new, but Scripture's personification of Wisdom has long played an important role for various groups in Judaism and early Christianity. Eastern Christians in particular have made perceptive use of Sophia in the church's iconography and theological traditions. Western Christianity has only recently joined this conversation. As Leo Lefebure notes, "Current disputes over the place of Sophia in Christian prayer and worship take place against the backdrop of a long and sometimes contentious history."[30]

Part of the strong reaction to the use of the name Sophia is due to fear that worship is being offered to a different god—that somehow Yahweh is being displaced by some sort of pagan goddess. In reality, the discomfort arises because tradition has had difficulty allowing the feminine to be too closely associated with the divine in the Jewish and Christian traditions; deity has been clothed in predominantly masculine attire in Christian theology, even though biblical texts continually challenge that limitation.

Spirit and Wisdom are closely related in the earliest christological interpretations, as we will see in the next chapter. The Logos tradition, given its masculine cast, was allowed to eclipse a Sophia Christology. Word and Wisdom as reciprocal expressions of Spirit rarely have been able to coexist in the literature or interpretation.

PROMISING A MESSIAH

The biblical narrative of the Spirit's power and presence portrays the various ways that God draws near to the beloved creation. While all participate in the movement of God's Spirit in the world and God's Spirit is active in all creaturely activity, the Hebrew Scriptures point to an even fuller indwelling than that experienced by the varied leaders of the gathered people of God. An anointed one will come; God's own messiah, upon whom the Spirit will rest, will make straight the path for those exiled from God. Multiple texts adumbrate the promised one (e.g., Isaiah 11:1-10; 42:1-4; Micah 5:1-6). Rather than speaking through the wavering courage of prophets, ruling through questionable monarchs, and teaching through world-weary sages, God's Spirit will reveal divine presence by sharing the status of "frail children of dust" as their messiah.

Spirit constitutes messianic identity. God chooses and authorizes the messiah by making him the bearer of the Spirit in an unprecedented way. In the words of Welker, "For the bringer of salvation, God's Spirit is an enduring endowment."[31] Justice and peace will be established because the Spirit has come to rest on this promised savior (Isaiah 61:1).

The Spirit will not empower the messiah to conquer enemies by supernatural force; rather, his woundedness will heal those who oppose him, as a messianic appropriation of Isaiah 53 suggests. Recently I heard Jean Vanier, founder of the L'Arche communities, which are comprised of mentally handicapped adults and those who choose to share residential life with them, offer a moving reflection on the way in which we are healed through the rejected other.[32] We must not presume to help the "poor other" from a position unaware of our own poverty, he suggested. Rather, it is in the power of those whom we might despise to convert us to see our own need and disability. We prefer to hide our faces from those whose lives seem such a graphic contrast to our own; yet when we allow them to claim our attention, we see our kinship to them and the ways in which we share life's exigencies.

The Spirit's presence in the messianic servant who suffers will not compel belief. The question of the source of power for his ministry will never be far from the lips of his detractors or his followers. How the messiah chooses to exercise power—gentle, humble ways that make room for the emancipatory actions of others—will not impress those who are looking for clearer demonstrations of the Spirit's anointing. They will want him to "lift his voice in the streets," to judge decisively those whose faith flickers, to perform signs that prove him to be "full of Spirit" (see Isaiah 42:1-4). As Welker perceptively writes, the messiah "does not choose the usual forms and strategies for acquiring moral and political attention and loyalty."[33]

What marks out the unique indwelling of the Spirit in the messiah? The obvious answer is that he is open to God and to others, receiving and giving love abundant. The less obvious answer

51

is that he is the bearer of the fresh wind of the Spirit blowing through all regnant structures, destabilizing patterns that stifle divine breath. Remarkably, the messiah makes no claim to divine prerogative, yet expresses the very will and life of God in human form. He realizes that his life is not self-generated, but is a participation in a larger reality by which he is borne along. He receives empowering *ruach* that allows a new meeting of God and humanity, sharing an embodied life. His life provides the template for how God intends all to join God's perichoretic movement in the world.

We have traced the presence of Spirit in gathering and forming a people in this chapter. Now we must explore further how Spirit empowers the messiah as God's own invitation to join in the dance.

NOTES

1. George A. Maloney, *The Spirit Broods Over the World* (New York: Alba House, 1993), 41.

2. Many biblical stories illustrate this tension. One of the most familiar in the Hebrew Scriptures is the narrative of Moses seeking to lead the recalcitrant people toward the land of promise.

3. Michael Welker, *God the Spirit*, trans. John F. Hoffmeyer (Minneapolis: Fortress, 1994), 65.

4. George T. Montague, *Holy Spirit: Growth of a Biblical Tradition* (Peabody, Mass.: Hendrickson, 1976), 18.

5. Welker, *God the Spirit*, 66.

6. Cf. the texts that identify Samson as one dedicated to God as a Nazirite: Judges 13:5,7; 16:17.

7. Welker, *God the Spirit*, 62–63.

8. Ulrich Simon offers a sustained theological reflection on the challenge of finding a horizon of promise in the atrocities of Auschwitz in *A Theology of Auschwitz* (London: SPCK, 1978).

9. This is true even (especially?) of Jesus. His inaugural sermon in Nazareth, as narrated in Luke 4, arouses not only suspicion, but also fury at his audacious claims.

10. Montague writes, "God is just in withdrawing his spirit because of Saul's infidelity. David's story shows that God is merciful and may freely decide not

to withdraw his gifts and his spirit" (*Holy Spirit*, 22).

11. Alasdair I. C. Heron, *The Holy Spirit* (Philadelphia: Westminster, 1983), 5.

12. Ibid.

13. I use this ambiguous designation to illustrate the difficulty of distinguishing divine spirit from human spirit, not to mention evil spirit, in many biblical texts.

14. Gary D. Badcock, *Light of Truth and Fire of Love: A Theology of the Holy Spirit* (Grand Rapids: Eerdmans, 1997), 18.

15. I will deal more thoroughly with the relationship between God and Moses in chapter 6.

16. Recent feminist scholarship has attempted to redress the neglect of Miriam in most standard commentaries and theologies of the Hebrew Scriptures. See especially the article by Phyllis Trible, "Bringing Miriam Out of the Shadows," *Bible Review* 5 (Fall 1989): 14–25, 34.

17. St. Gregory the Great makes a similar point: "Holy men were never able to hand on to others the miraculous powers which they received from God" (*Life and Miracles of St. Benedict*, trans. Odo J. Zimmermann and Benedict R. Avery [Collegeville, Minn.: Liturgical Press, 1949], 26).

18. Montague, *Holy Spirit*, 28.

19. Welker, *God the Spirit*, 65.

20. Gordon W. Lathrop, *Holy Things: A Liturgical Theology* (Minneapolis: Fortress, 1993), esp. 119–124.

21. Don E. Saliers notes the spiritual significance of the Psalter in formative worship: "In every age of renewal . . . the Psalms have provided a foundation for both the people's sung prayer in the liturgical assembly and the composition of hymns" ("Singing Our Lives," in *Practicing Our Faith: A Way of Life for a Searching People*, ed. Dorothy C. Bass [San Francisco: Jossey-Bass, 1997], 186).

22. Christine D. Pohl identifies the practice of hospitality as a distinctive characteristic of Israel (*Making Room: Recovering Hospitality as a Christian Tradition* [Grand Rapids: Eerdmans, 1999], 23–29). Cf. Hans Walter Wolff, *Anthropology of the Old Testament* (Philadelphia: Fortress, 1975), 188.

23. These perceptive words of dialectic are from Miroslav Volf. See his *Exclusion and Embrace: A Theological Exploration of Identity, Otherness, and Reconciliation* (Nashville: Abingdon, 1996).

24. Mark I. Wallace, *Fragments of the Spirit: Nature, Violence, and the Renewal of Creation* (New York: Continuum, 1996), 201.

25. Wallace, *Fragments of the Spirit*, 202.

26. Badcock, *Light of Truth*, 13.

27. Walter Brueggemann, *Theology of the Old Testament: Testimony, Dispute, Advocacy* (Minneapolis: Fortress, 1997), 680–681.

28. Michael E. Lodahl, *Shekhinah/Spirit: Divine Presence in Jewish and Christian Religion* (New York: Paulist Press, 1992), 49.

29. Nearly a decade after the Re-imagining Conference (held in Minneapolis in the fall of 1993 as a part of an Ecumenical Decade of Churches in Solidarity with Women, an initiative of the World Council of Churches), many still think that an alternative God—Sophia—was proposed to displace the God revealed in Scripture. The conference had simply recovered the biblical vision of the personification of Wisdom, one of the means of God's self-expression in Scripture. For further reflection, see "ABC Leaders Respond to Women's Conference," *Christian Century* 111, no. 11 (April 6, 1994): 345, and Joseph D. Small and John P. Burgess, "Evaluating 'Re-Imagining,'" *Christian Century* 111, no. 11 (April 6, 1994): 342–344.

30. Leo Lefebure, "The Wisdom of God: Sophia and Christian Theology," *Christian Century* 111, no. 29 (October 19, 1994): 951.

31. Welker, *God the Spirit*, 109.

32. On October 25, 2000, Jean Vanier received the Dignitas Humana award from the School of Theology at St. John's University. He presented these ideas throughout his day of lectures.

33. Welker, *God the Spirit*, 125.

CHAPTER 4

EMPOWERING THE CHRIST

The Spirit of the Lord *God is upon me,*
because the Lord *has anointed me.*
—*Isaiah 61:1*

Then Jesus, filled with the power of the Spirit,
returned to Galilee.
—*Luke 4:14*

THE FORMULATION OF THE EARLIEST CREEDS STILL, IN LARGE MEAS-
ure, dictates our understanding of the triune God, and particularly our pneumatology. Historically, the doctrine of the Spirit
has been outlined subsequent to the affirmations concerning
Christ. The order of the articles in the earliest statements of faith
suggests a linear chronology to the self-revealing of God in the
threefold Trinitarian history embedded in Scripture.[1] Generations
of faithful Christians have reaffirmed this time-honored order as
they confess their faith: We believe (1) in God almighty; (2) and
in Jesus Christ, his only Son, our Lord; (3) and in the Holy Spirit.
The earliest summary statement, the Apostles' Creed, mentions
the Spirit only in conjunction with the birth of the Son, who was
"conceived of the Holy Spirit, born of the Virgin Mary."[2] It was
not until the fourth-century Nicene Creed that the Spirit is
described as "Lord and the Life-giver."[3] Prior to that, there was
considerable debate about ascribing divinity to the Spirit. Part of
the reticence to do so had to do with the New Testament's spare
language about the Spirit; in only one text is the Spirit given the
title "Lord" (2 Corinthians 3:18). Another reason for this neglect

is that these first centuries had as their most pressing concern the contours of the relation between the other members of the Trinity, the Father and the Son.[4]

This creedal order, in which the Spirit comes last and is treated with expedient dispatch, intimates that the Spirit was not present, at least not in an encompassing way, until after Christ ascended. Pentecost thus marks the coming of the Spirit. Our study of the Hebrew Scriptures suggests, however, that awareness of the presence of the divine as Spirit was already constitutive of the religious experiences of the people of God long before the advent of the messiah. They knew God preeminently as Spirit whose power was displayed throughout nature and whose presence was intimately experienced by those who longed for God. Furthermore, the literature of the Hebrew Scriptures portrays a reciprocal, dynamic relationship obtaining between Spirit and Word and Wisdom—key modes of divine presence—a relationship that is further refined in the New Testament.

In the preceding chapter we explored how the Spirit makes possible the gathering of a people inspirited for God's use and their own vitality. Now we must turn to an investigation of how the Spirit empowers the Christ to make God present with us, as one of us. Only in light of this Christological analysis will the Spirit's work of birthing the church make sense, as the next chapter explicates.

We cannot understand the identity of Jesus of Nazareth apart from the movement of the Spirit in his life and in the lives of those receptive to the new wind blowing through their very souls, stirring them to recognize God's messiah. Awaiting the Spirit in power was a part of the realization of the messianic age,[5] but this does not mean that God's power as Spirit was not already evident in the faith of Israel. Yet something new does occur: Jesus and the Spirit are mutually interpreted in terms of promise and fulfillment for the people of God.

The Evangelists understood that the story of Jesus must be told amidst the stories of those upon whom his ministry depends— for example, Mary, John the Baptist, Simeon and Anna, and his many followers and friends. Their receptivity to this new movement of God in the history of their people was a necessary part of Jesus' own recognition that he was being propelled by the Spirit "to fulfill all righteousness" (Matthew 3:15).

Examining the life of Jesus as a work of the Spirit allows us to see both the uniqueness of God's initiative in him and the commonality of his life with ours as together we participate in the life of God. Furthermore, we learn how his life can be formed in us by the power of the Spirit.

OVERSHADOWING HUMANITY

Scripture associates the presence of Spirit with expressions of God's power, indeed with life itself. Nothing has come into being apart from the vivifying presence of the breath of God. The brooding Spirit, hovering over the waters of chaos, is a portrait of the birthing of new life. Other scenes come to mind: the dove searching for life in the receding waters of the flood (Genesis 8:8-12), the Spirit "coming upon" Mary (Luke 1:35), and the descending winged One at the baptism of Jesus (Mark 1:10 pars.). This hovering presence is a recurring image in the Bible, as Spirit communicates God's creative intent, overshadowing nature's chaotic bent.

The semantic range of the word *overshadow* is considerable. It can mean, in its more vigorous sense, "overwhelming," "strong," "intense," "uncontrollable," "nearly eclipsing;" in its more subtle sense, it can mean "comforting, evocative presence," "forbearing power," and "encompassing attendance." As used in the Bible,[6] overshadowing conveys the idea of an intensely powerful experience of the presence of God. The Septuagint uses *episkiazō* ("overshadow") to describe the cloud over the tabernacle (Exodus 40:35; cf.

skiazō in Numbers 9:18,22), a visual representation of the descent of God's glorious presence, and to speak of God's unwavering protection and favor (Psalm 90:4; 139:8).

The same word occurs in several New Testament texts: the transfiguration story (Mark 9:7; Matthew 17:5; Luke 9:34), which sustains the earlier cloud imagery; the narrative of the annunciation to Mary (Luke 1:35), where the connotation is one of immanent, glorious presence and protection; and the traditions about the healing shadow of Peter (Acts 5:15), a powerful bearer of Spirit since Pentecost. Overshadowing is an apt description of the presence of Spirit—at times so concentrated as to be almost overwhelming, yet still allowing space and opportunity for creaturely action. As evocative presence, Spirit calls forth wonder, praise, and trust. As "weight of glory,"[7] the impress of holy presence is felt deeply.

The most familiar usage of the word *overshadow* is in the annunciation story. Here it becomes a description of how the Spirit will empower Mary to bring forth the very Son of God. Reminiscent of the Spirit's beginning creative work, bringing form out of the void, the Spirit calls forth life from the emptiness of Mary's womb. Raymond Brown calls this a "surprise of creation."[8] The birth of Jesus surpasses the human request and divine fulfillment seen in the story of the birth of his forerunner John the Baptist. Contrary to the birth of John, "this is God's initiative going beyond anything man or woman has dreamed of."[9] The birth of the Son, moreover, is a collaboration of human and divine. The conception requires both the Spirit's fecundity and Mary's fruitful yes.

How we construe the Spirit's overshadowing of Mary is a delicate matter theologically. While we affirm that Jesus is born like every other child, we believe that the doctrine of the "virginal conception" safeguards the divine initiative in his coming to life. Nevertheless, it is not necessary to highlight the Spirit's work at the expense of Mary, as Jürgen Moltmann does in *The Way of*

Jesus Christ, in order to buttress his pneumatological Christology.[10] Moltmann's diminishment of Mary is described by Beverly Gaventa as "Protestant minimalism."[11] She contends that Moltmann accords to the Spirit traditional Christian reflection about Mary, thus making the Spirit, in his words, "the great virginal, life-engendering mother of all the living, and as such the divine archetype of Mary, the mother of Jesus Christ."[12] Mary often has been subsumed into the larger discussion of the work of the Spirit in conceiving the Christ. Important as it is to accent this unique work of the Spirit, Mary's role must not be eclipsed. Indeed, God waited for her response, her voluntary collaboration. In her poem "Annunciation," Denise Levertov notes the importance of Mary's yes to God. She could have said no, a "choice integral to humanness."[13]

Leonardo Boff moves in the opposite direction from Moltmann as he accords characteristics of Spirit to Mary, thereby moving her toward divinization. Boff writes "I would say that the Holy Spirit, coming down on Mary, 'pneumatized' her, taking on human form in her, in the same manner as the Son who, in personal and unmistakable manner, set up his tent amongst us in the figure of Jesus of Nazareth."[14] As might be expected of a Catholic scholar who is seeking to find a feminine face for God, Boff uses language of Mary usually reserved for the incarnate Son. The approach of neither Moltmann nor Boff will suffice. We cannot divinize Mary, nor can we minimize the contribution of her human collaboration with God. The virginal conception is a divine-human action. The Spirit's overshadowing does not obliterate the significance of human participation. Birth, whether physical or spiritual, does not occur apart from or in spite of flesh. Rather, flesh is a prime locus for the Spirit's dwelling and the necessary medium of divine manifestation. Overshadowing, thus, is not unilateral divine action; God's creative movement accords with the receptive participation of the human partner.

Mary's interrogation of the annunciation is straightforward: how is it possible to conceive a child without "knowing a man" (Luke 1:34)? Gabriel is equally forthright, even if it is to give an unprecedented description of where babies come from: "The Holy Spirit will come upon you, and the power of the Most High will overshadow you" (Luke 1:35).

God's favor toward Mary is recognized by others who move to the cadences of the Spirit. Filled with the Spirit, Elizabeth prophetically identifies Mary as the "mother of my Lord" (Luke 1:43), and Zechariah understands the birth of his son as integral to God's salvation, as he will "go before the Lord to prepare [the way]" (Luke 1:76).

The Spirit is God's means of overshadowing humanity. In the biblical narrative, God's merciful nearness continually calls forth new life. When the Spirit of God overshadows, the improbable, indeed the seemingly impossible, occurs. Dry bones become a renewed people in a flourishing land, a virginal rose blooms with child, and a young man of questionable background is commissioned to the vocation of messiah.

ANOINTING FOR MINISTRY

In the preceding chapter we began exploring how Spirit is related to messianic identity. We observed how messiah was closely associated with Spirit in the Hebrew Scriptures. The word *anoint* used of the Spirit in Isaiah 61:1 is of the same root as *messiah*.[15] Spirit comes to new expression in the life of Jesus of Nazareth as one anointed by divine presence. Elizabeth Johnson sums up this relation: "According to the witness of Scripture, Jesus is a genuine Spirit-phenomenon, conceived, inspired, sent, hovered over, guided, and risen from the dead by her power."[16] The promised one will have the Spirit resting upon him; his anointing for ministry will be the outpouring of the Spirit.

The Gospels extend the prophetic imagery of the Spirit being offered in unprecedented fashion to God's servant (e.g., Isaiah 42:1; 59:21; 61:1). We have already noted how the conception of Jesus is pictured as an enigmatic expression of the infilling of the Spirit. The narrative portrayal of the baptism of Jesus furthers this imagery of the Spirit's anointing for ministry. In the scene of Jesus being baptized by John, all four Gospels portray the descent of the Spirit in the figure of a dove accompanied by a voice, which, in the Synoptic portrayals, says, "You are [Matthew: 'This is'] my beloved son, in whom I have delight" (Mark 1:11, pars.). The descent of the Spirit continues the theme of over-shadowing by the divine presence. Jesus is marked out as an instrument of the Spirit at every stage of his life.

There has been much scholarly discussion on the depiction of the Spirit as a dove both in Scripture and in visual representations in Christian art.[17] Some have contended that the dove is a feminine symbol that ameliorates the masculinist cast of the scene at the Jordan. Early Syrian Christianity gives most attention to the feminization of Spirit, primarily in liturgical prayer.[18] Although this Eastern Christian tradition rightly claimed a certain aptness to using feminine metaphors for the Spirit, it also understood the limits of speaking of God in this manner. Certain feminine activities and symbols were linked to the Spirit—for example, birthing, cleansing, and midwifing. While this is understandable, it perpetuates a stereotyping of feminine roles.

Assigning literal feminine gender to the Spirit opens the door to assigning literal masculine gender to God,[19] thus creating, in my judgment, insuperable problems. Gavin D'Costa says it well: "To see the Spirit as feminine therefore ironically highlights the patriarchal taxonomies of representation that have tended to exist in both east and west."[20] More important is to affirm that the whole of messianic promise realized in Jesus is empowered by Spirit, who, as God, transcends gender. Gender attribution to God is never to be understood literally,[21] as that is to confuse human and divine being. It is fitting, in some contexts, to use gendered allusions to remind us that personal imagery is useful in thinking about God.

We have seen how Spirit and Wisdom are almost used interchangeably in the Hebrew Scriptures. For example, the messianic traditions envision the coming one as endowed with Wisdom and Spirit. Isaiah 11:1-2 is a critical text in this regard: "A shoot shall come out from the stump of Jesse, and a branch shall grow out of his roots. The spirit of the LORD shall rest on him, the spirit of wisdom and understanding, the spirit of counsel and might, the spirit of knowledge and the fear of the LORD." The New Testament continues this pattern as it employs these expressions of divine presence to delineate the empowering of Christ, yet a heightened focus on Word threatens to sever the threads that connect messianic identity with Wisdom and Spirit.

In the earliest New Testament Christological constructions, Jesus is described as an expression of Wisdom/Spirit; only later is he identified as Word. The eliding of Sophia and Spirit had already occurred in the deuterocanonical text Wisdom 7:22-23,27. Elisabeth Schüssler Fiorenza argues that the language of Jewish wisdom theology provides the interpretative framework for the earliest attempts to understand the significance of the ministry of Jesus.[22] This is a helpful insight that we must attend to as we seek to construct a pneumatic Christology.

Why does this technical distinction between Wisdom/Spirit and Word Christologies matter? Are not both equally biblical approaches to understanding the identity of Jesus within the context of messianic expectation? If we are to understand a reciprocal relationship between Jesus and the Spirit, a relationship in which Spirit is both the giver and the gift of the Christ, then it matters a great deal. Logos Christology, which originated with the Alexandrine theologians,[23] has been a predominant interest for many years and usually tends toward a subordinate theology of Spirit.[24] Word becomes the determinative category, and Wisdom is silenced. Understanding the ministry of Jesus from the perspective of Hebrew scriptural Wisdom teaching has several advantages over against an exclusive focus on the Word. First, when Logos subsumes Christological interpretations, Spirit as vivifying presence is subdued. Second, the Logos emphasis of the Fourth Gospel moves in the semantic field of "Father-Son" language, which opens the door to merging "the biological masculine gender of Jesus and the grammatical masculine gender of Logos."[25] The outcome of this logic is that the "masculine" Word is retrojected into the being of God as eternal Son.

This discussion raises the difficult question of the nature of incarnation. Is something essentially male expressed as "word made flesh," with the concomitant necessity of a male embodiment? Peter Hodgson offers a piercing critique of the liabilities of the "Logos-flesh" Christology. Here I highlight three of his criticisms germane to the present argument: (1) "It personifies or hypostatizes the Logos, regarding him as a gendered divine agent"; (2) "It reifies Jesus' maleness (his contingent human particularity) into an ontological quality of Christ and God"; (3) "Incarnationist christology thinks in terms not of relations or actions but of a duality of divine and human 'natures,' hierarchically distinguished from each other."[26]

These are vigorous challenges to the classical tradition, and, for the most part, well taken. Contemporary people simply do not use the ancient philosophical categories of substance and nature when speaking about Jesus. Hence, close inspection of the creeds leaves many people confused or, worse, dispassionate about the subject of the humanity and divinity of Christ.

The pneumatology that I have been seeking to articulate allows us to perceive the identity of Jesus as the embodiment of the Spirit, fully indwelt and empowered by God's own presence, yet without the concrete personal self of Jesus being displaced by the divine.

Too often when we begin to speak about incarnation, the Trinity is neatly compartmentalized: the First and Third Persons remain in heaven, while the Second Person, the Son, descends to inhabit human form. Relocating and dismembering the being of God in this fashion, with its curious spatial arrangement, does violence to the ways in which God expresses presence as Spirit and Son in the creation. Furthermore, it displays an antiquated cosmology that interpreters would employ in no other sphere of understanding.

Rather than speaking of incarnation as a portion of God that was simply "veiled in flesh," disguised as a human, it is more helpful to use the biblical description: "In him the whole fullness of deity dwells bodily" (Colossians 2:9). This construction suggests a pouring out and a filling up, a movement between emptiness and fullness, a dance of human and divine life; a unique life embedded in the story of God and in the story of humanity.[27] Eastern Orthodox theologians often characterize Spirit as that expression of God which opens the divine life outward to all that is not God.[28] Spirit overshadows and anoints Jesus as Christ; one who is human, not God, becomes the very expression of God in the world. Spirit, dancing through the life of Jesus, empowers him to be the "lord of the dance."

INAUGURATING THE REIGN

The reign of God is central to understanding the ministry of Jesus. His proclamation, his prophetic signs, and his very person express the nearness of God. While it is tempting to devote much time to the ministry of Jesus inaugurating the reign of God, the heart of this study is the trajectory of Spirit as God's embrace and empowerment of all creation. Although we are looking through a Christological lens in this chapter, it is for the purpose of illuminating the function of Spirit as the mode of God's presence in this human life and to gain clues about God's movement in all human life. Viewing the life of Jesus primarily as a work of the Spirit creates a bridge to our interpretation of our lives as living icons that are also bearers of Spirit.

Through the description of the origin of Jesus the Christ as a divine-human collaboration, born of water and of the Spirit, we have already begun to speak of his uniqueness. Overshadowed even prior to his birth, he is the one in whom Spirit resides in an unprecedented manner; he is also the one through whom the Spirit works in unhindered freedom.

But first he is tested. From the comforting commissioning at the Jordan to the searing silence of the desert, the Spirit drives the Christ toward the precipice of unknowing. As Patricia Farris puts it, "The same Holy Spirit who gave Jesus life has led him to the Place of Devastation, that he might be tested."[29] Drawing from Barbara Brown Taylor, William Willimon observes, "Here is no sweet dove. This Spirit thing has claws, talons."[30]

Sorting out the temptations that Jesus faced is not our main concern at this point; besides, I think that we know them pretty well in contemporary dress. How will we ensure our safety in a time of terror? How will we secure our needs as fragile, embodied humans who need bread? How will we align ourselves politically as citizens who can escape neither God nor Caesar? Will we trust God, or bombs, the stock market, and the "right people" in office?

More demanding for our consideration is the question of what it means to discern the way of Spirit in a world that demands material proof. How can we sniff out "lying words that sound religious"[31]—the adversary's choice vocabulary? We are always tempted to demand that God provide certified proof of divine presence with us, and it is never enough for our rationalistic appetites.

We have grown accustomed to thinking of the Spirit in terms of comfort and security, and are tempted to flee the difficult and demanding as surely not being God's will for us, the favored. The Gospel texts that narrate the testing of Jesus (Matthew 4:1-11;

Luke 4:1-13) demand that we think of the Spirit in terms of rending decisions that are not so clear, utter reliance on what does not seem reasonable, and a sheer willingness not to presume competence where we are novices.

Being led by the Spirit is hazardous duty, requiring that Jesus and all who follow him be honest about themselves. We are faced with the same questions that the devil hurled at Jesus, and we are not sure how to respond. Ironically, the questions of temptation may also be the questions of discernment. We long to give our lives in vocation that pleases God and serves humanity, but we know all too well our weakness. We are perplexed by how far to stretch the boundaries of the people of God, especially when it means that people are too suspicious of us to join hands with us.

Being led by the Spirit will put us at odds with our culture of deceit, at odds with some of our Christian brothers and sisters who are quick to denounce as morally wrong that which makes them uncomfortable. And following the Spirit will require of us faith—all the guidance we usually get is enough to take the next uncertain step. Moltmann puts it this way: "The road emerged only as I walked it."[32] So it was in the life of Jesus.

When questioned about the source of empowerment for his ministry, Jesus clearly points to the Spirit. On one occasion, some Pharisees suggested that he performed exorcisms by the power of evil. Rejecting that insinuation and warning of the danger of not being able to identify power that comes from God, he contended that such mighty acts are a demonstration that the Spirit is inaugurating the *basileia tou theou*: "If it is by the Spirit of God that I cast out demons, then the kingdom of God has come to you" (Matthew 12:28).

Luke's Gospel most clearly attests that Jesus' ministry was thoroughly empowered by the Spirit. From the inaugural sermon in Nazareth (Luke 4:16-27) to the final breath on the cross (Luke 23:46), the Spirit voices liberation and hope, healing and forgiveness, through Jesus the Christ. The mighty acts that he performs are expressions of the radical reversals that will characterize the reign of God. Anointed by the Spirit, Jesus brings good news to the poor, proclaims release for the captive, recovery of sight for the blind, and freedom for the oppressed, and declares the year of the Lord's favor to all (Luke 4:18-19). In the power of the Spirit, Jesus the Messiah demonstrates that God's reign is already beginning to flourish.

The reign of God exposes all illusions of human self-reliance. Even Jesus the Christ must depend upon power from God to be faithful to his calling. He counsels his followers not to depend upon their own skills or perceptions; he had learned for himself the truth that only in the power of the Spirit could he do the work of the one who had sent him. As John's Gospel puts it, "He whom God has sent speaks the words of God, for [God] gives the Spirit without measure" (John 3:34). Spirit-empowered word is expressed through frail flesh. Flesh and Spirit, while not in opposition, have their limitations when severed. Jesus' statement to Nicodemus, "What is born of the flesh is flesh, and what is born of the Spirit is spirit" (John 3:6), points to the encompassing sphere of God's movement.[33] The Spirit empowers flesh to do far beyond its finite capacity.

The activities of the reign inaugurated by the Spirit are best interpreted as the practice of compassion. Marcus Borg suggests that Spirit and compassion are central to understanding Jesus.[34] We have already considered how Spirit empowers Jesus' enactment of God's reign. Now we must consider how that reign stunningly displays Jesus' "politics of compassion," as Borg describes the character of his ministry.[35]

Scene after scene in the Gospels depicts the compassion of Jesus. Touching lepers (Matthew 8:3), mingling with the unclean (Mark 5:27), welcoming children (Mark 10:14), lodging with the despised (Luke 19:7), straightening bent bodies (Luke 13:13)—Jesus' compassion is evident in self-expending actions. Compassion is a way of being with others, bearing their suffering with them. Compassion does not try to heal or comfort from a distance; rather, its willingness to wade into the thick of it with others means putting the self at risk. This Jesus does, without regard for the looming crisis.

The Servant Songs of Isaiah had long before described the sturdy compassion of the one upon whom God puts the Spirit. The Servant would not break the "bruised reed" or quench the "dimly burning wick" (Isaiah 42:3)—symbols of a downtrodden people whose faith flickers in doubt. In humility, God's Servant would rather receive physical suffering than inflict it (Isaiah 50:6). His compassion compels him to bear the sufferings of others that they might be healed, as the fourth song in the cycle graphically portrays: "Surely he has borne our infirmities and carried our diseases; yet we accounted him stricken, struck down by God, and afflicted. But he was wounded for our transgressions, crushed for our iniquities; upon him was the punishment that made us whole, and by his bruises we are healed" (Isaiah 53:4-5).

The Spirit-inspired compassion of Jesus the Messiah brings him to insurmountable conflict with religious and civil authorities. He is charged with being a threat to the stability of both the temple system and the state. Hence, an unholy alliance of religious and political leaders conspires to do away with him. And they succeed—or so it seemed as the light was eclipsed on that fateful Friday that we call "good."

SUSTAINING THROUGH DEATH

How does Jesus die and yet live? It is by the power of the Spirit of God. The breath of God, temporarily withdrawn in the abandoning of the Son, returns as the Spirit recreates life, stirring the Christ toward reunion with the Sending One and the scattered disciples.

It is exceedingly difficult to speak of the experience of the triune God in the event of the cross, for issues of the suffering of God, as well as death in the life of God, are wrapped in mystery. The relation of deity and humanity is strained to the breaking point in the delivering up of the Son, the cry of forsakenness, and the release of Spirit. Theologians have attempted to examine this complex event through the lens of the distinctive members of the Trinity, primarily focusing on the experience of the Father and the Son. Insufficient attention, however, has been devoted to the sustaining power of the Spirit, through whom the being of God retains its perichoretic union. This union is interrupted, threatened, and is forced to receive within its essential life that which is other than God—death, separation, and the abyss of sin.

How does the Spirit sustain the dance of giving and receiving when even death enters the divine movement? The overshadowing Spirit absorbs within the divine life the rending of relationships and transforms the seeming end into beginning. The Spirit not only gives life to all creation, but also gives new life within and beyond death. The crucified is not utterly abandoned, but is, in the words of Johnson, gathered "into new transformed life, promise of a future for all the dead and the whole cosmos itself."[36]

The association of the Spirit with the resurrection of Jesus Christ does not appear explicitly in the Gospels, but is to be found in Acts and in the Epistles. For example, Romans 1:4-5 refers to Jesus as designated "Son of God with power according to the spirit of holiness by resurrection from the dead, Jesus Christ our Lord, through whom we have received grace and apostleship." A confession in 1 Timothy 3:16 includes the words "he was manifested in the flesh, vindicated in the Spirit," the latter phrase being a reference to the resurrection. First Peter 3:18 speaks of Christ being "put to death in the flesh, but made alive in the spirit," while Romans 8:11 states the matter explicitly: "If the Spirit of [the One] who raised Jesus from the dead dwells in you, [the One] who raised Christ from the dead will give life to your mortal bodies also through [the] Spirit [who] dwells in you." Resurrection occurs in the power of the Spirit.

Rarely has the proclamation of the church included all the distinctive accents of Scripture concerning resurrection. Usually it has been interpreted too much in the past tense (focused on what occurred on Easter morning), too individualistically, and with little regard for how the resurrection of Jesus Christ needs to be interpreted in the larger horizon of God's holistic resurrecting movement. We must address this challenge in the final chapters.

NOTES

1. Jürgen Moltmann offers a sustained argument for the biblical warrant for Trinitarian theology. See his section on Trinitarian hermeneutics in *The Trinity and the Kingdom: The Doctrine of God*, trans. Margaret Kohl (San Francisco: Harper & Row, 1981), 61–75.

2. Cited in Henry Bettenson, ed., *Documents of the Christian Church*, 2nd ed. (Oxford: Oxford University Press, 1963), 24.

3. Ibid., 26. Most of the Nicene Creed of 325 is preoccupied with the Christological matters in the face of the Arian controversy. Hence, article two on Christ is lengthy, detailing the origin and nature of the Son, his life, death, resurrection, ascension, heavenly session, and promised return. In contrast, the statement on the Spirit is brief, almost an afterthought. Indeed, the rise of the "Pneumatomachoi" (opponents of the Spirit) in the 380s demonstrates the consequences of the pneumatological omission. See James Stevenson and W. H. C. Frend, eds., *Creeds, Councils, and Controversies: Documents Illustrating the History of the Church A.D. 337–461*, rev. ed. (London: SPCK, 1989).

4. Once again I revert to the traditional language, for this is the language of these early formulations. See the argument later in this chapter that counters this naming of God.

5. Gordon D. Fee, *God's Empowering Presence: The Holy Spirit in The Letters of Paul* (Peabody, Mass.: Hendrickson, 1994), 4.

6. For this lexical work I am drawing from Horst Balz and Gerhard Schneider, eds., *Exegetical Dictionary of the New Testament*, vol. 2 (Grand Rapids: Eerdmans, 1991), 34–35.

7. *Kabod* is a Hebrew word for "glory," which connotes the heaviness of divine presence.

8. Raymond E. Brown, *The Birth of the Messiah: A Commentary on the*

Infancy Narratives in Matthew and Luke (Garden City, N.Y.: Doubleday, 1977), 314.

9. Ibid.

10. Jürgen Moltmann, *The Way of Jesus Christ: Christology in Messianic Dimensions,* trans. Margaret Kohl (San Francisco: HarperSanFrancisco, 1990), 73.

11. Beverly R. Gaventa, *Mary: Glimpses of the Mother of Jesus* (Minneapolis: Fortress, 1999), 17.

12. Moltmann, *Way of Jesus Christ,* 84.

13. Denise Levertov, *The Stream and the Sapphire: Selected Poems on Religious Themes* (New York: New Directions, 1997), 59.

14. Leonardo Boff, *Trinity and Society,* trans. Paul Burns (Maryknoll, N.Y.: Orbis, 1988), 210–211.

15. This link is preserved in Greek in the words for "Christ" and "anoint" with the Spirit in Acts 4:26.

16. Elizabeth A. Johnson, *She Who Is: The Mystery of God in Feminist Theological Discourse* (New York: Crossroad, 1992), 150.

17. See the discussion by Gavin D'Costa, *Sexing the Trinity: Gender, Culture and the Divine* (London: SCM, 2000), 183–186. Also helpful in understanding the larger setting of liturgical symbols in early Christian art is Robin Margaret Jensen, *Understanding Early Christian Art* (New York: Routledge, 2000).

18. To my knowledge, the best source for this discussion is by Susan Ashbrook Harvey, "Feminine Image for the Divine: The Holy Spirit, the Odes of Solomon and Early Syriac Tradition," *St. Vladimir's Theological Quarterly* 37 (1993): 111–139.

19. For perceptive insights on the challenge of applying the category of gender to God, see David S. Cunningham, *These Three Are One: The Practice of Trinitarian Theology* (Oxford: Blackwell, 1998), 46–49.

20. D'Costa, *Sexing the Trinity,* 11.

21. Ibid., 46.

22. Elisabeth Schüssler Fiorenza, *Jesus: Miriam's Child, Sophia's Prophet: Critical Issues in Feminist Christology* (New York: Continuum, 1994), 140.

23. See the significant analysis of this tradition by Aloys Grillmeier, *Christ in Christian Tradition,* vol. 1, trans. John Bowden, rev. ed. (Atlanta: John Knox, 1975), 133–149.

24. For example, Martin Hengel, *The Son of God: The Origin of Christology and the History of Jewish-Hellenistic Religion,* trans. John Bowden (Philadelphia: Fortress, 1976); Karl-Josef Kuschel, *Born Before All Time? The Dispute over Christ's Origin,* trans. John Bowden (London: SCM, 1992).

25. Schüssler Fiorenza, *Jesus,* 153.

26. Peter C. Hodgson, *Winds of the Spirit: A Constructive Christian Theology* (Louisville: Westminster John Knox, 1994), 248–249.

27. Kathryn Tanner interprets the humanity and divinity of Jesus in a

helpful way: "Better to think of divinity and humanity not in terms of isolable, discrete qualities that divide up Jesus' life and person, but as what characterize Jesus' life overall, as a whole" (*Jesus, Humanity, and the Trinity: A Brief Systematic Theology* [Minneapolis: Fortress, 2001], 16).

28. Tanner directed my attention to Dumitru Staaniloae, who illustrates this idea in *Theology and the Church*, trans. Robert Barringer (Crestwood, N.Y.: St. Vladimir's Seminary Press, 1980).

29. Patricia Farris, "Bedrock Truths," *Christian Century* 119, no. 3 (January 30, 2002): 18.

30. William Willimon, "Vocational Temptation," *Theology Today* 52, no. 1 (April 1995): 99.

31. David E. Garland, *Reading Matthew: A Literary and Theological Commentary on the First Gospel* (New York: Crossroad, 1993), 38.

32. Jürgen Moltmann, *Experiences in Theology: Ways and Forms of Christian Theology*, trans. Margaret Kohl (Minneapolis: Fortress, 2000), xv.

33. We should not interpret this Johannine passage in a docetic way. Pitting spirit against flesh is not in keeping with the tenor of "word made flesh," which informs the theology of the Fourth Gospel.

34. Marcus Borg, *Meeting Jesus Again for the First Time: The Historical Jesus and the Heart of Contemporary Faith* (San Francisco: HarperSanFrancisco, 1994), 46.

35. Marcus Borg, *Jesus, A New Vision: Spirit, Culture, and the Life of Discipleship* (San Francisco: Harper & Row, 1987).

36. Johnson, *She Who Is*, 159.

CHAPTER 5

BIRTHING THE CHURCH

And the disciples were filled with joy
and with the Holy Spirit.
—Acts 13:52

God's love has been poured into our hearts through
the Holy Spirit that has been given to us.
—Romans 5:5

WE NOW MOVE FROM EXAMINING THE CONCENTRATED EXPERIENCE
of Spirit in the life of Jesus to the new fullness of spiritual experience in the "discipleship of equals"—Elisabeth Schüssler
Fiorenza's evocative description of the embryonic church.[1]
Prior to the advent of the Christ, the Spirit was experienced in
a universal, creative sense, and also by individual leaders
indwelt for specific purposes. As we have observed, the filling
and abiding presence of the Spirit, linked to the messianic age,
had not yet occurred for all. The prophetic promise of an inclusive outpouring in which the Spirit would remain was drawing
near. The birthing work of the Spirit that flourished in the coming of the messiah now continues in conceiving a new corporate identity that expresses life with Christ in the power of the
Spirit. The means by which the resurrected Christ will be able
to remain where "two or three are gathered" (Matthew 18:20)
is in the Spirit.

In the preceding chapter we considered the Spirit as the life-
giver of Jesus of Nazareth, who was "God's Spirit in person."[2] In
the present chapter we trace the fecundity of the Spirit in giving

73

life to the body of Christ. There will necessarily be a mutuality of giving and receiving between the Spirit and the risen Lord as we trace the continuation of the Spirit's maternity. This reciprocity reminds us that we can participate in the life of God only through the "two hands"—Irenaeus's memorable image of Spirit and Son—that eternally extend God's embrace to the world. Christology and pneumatology come together in ecclesiology[3] as Spirit makes Christ ever present in the community gathered around the cross. The life poured out on the cross now fills the followers of Christ with living water that keeps spilling into the world. Life in the Spirit always pushes toward new forms of communal experience, in ever widening circles.

DELIVERING CHRISTIAN COMMUNITY

Community is a unifying theme in the history of the people of God, but the concept of community undergoes considerable development in the epochs reflected in Scripture.[4] The new community that gathered around Jesus during his life was shaped by his perspective on the reign of God, where the mighty and the lowly exchange places by the radical reordering of God's Spirit and all can find welcome. The vision of this reign incorporates familiar themes of the past, but bears the distinctive stamp of the pneumatic Christ, especially his receptivity toward the ministry and friendship of women and his iconoclastic challenge to patriarchal society in general.[5] As social-scientific studies of the New Testament have demonstrated, the entrenched *paterfamilias* structure marginalized many persons, not just women.[6] Thus the poor, the enslaved, and the outcast were all subjects of Jesus' advocacy.

Bruce Malina suggests that Jesus' proclamation of a new social order was directed to the "problem posed by Roman political economy as appropriated by local Israelite aristocracy."[7] In other words, some in Israel benefited from the foreign occupation of the land by oppressing their compatriots, which Jesus boldly challenged. Thus, the reign of God signaled a new option for the poor, as divine patronage would secure their lives against the violence of rigid class structures and their endemic personal control. Jesus cautions against using titles of rank or dominance (Matthew 23:8,10), as such distinctions not only set up insufferable hierarchies among people, but also displace the prerogatives of God. God alone is reliable to depend upon utterly.

Spirit-driven ministry has an inescapable public character to it—social, economic, and political. As Paul Hanson observes, because "Jesus and his followers refused to resolve the tension between God's order and the order of this world by a retreat into monastic communes,"[8] they could not avoid conflict—indeed, as Jesus cautioned, they should expect it (Luke 12:51-53). The public ministry of the Spirit-empowered Christ regularly evoked protests because he systematically challenged "establishment violence."[9]

Although there is some debate about the degree to which Jesus was willing to traverse the boundaries of Israel to invite Gentiles to participate in the realm of God,[10] certainly the springs of a universal gospel are evident in what Hanson calls his "openness of style."[11] These springs will well up into the gushing stream of Pentecost, when the Spirit will flow freely to all. We can see among the followers of Jesus the Messiah, even prior to the dramatic reorienting experiences in the upper room and on the streets of Jerusalem, a kind of inclusive community that stresses participation through repentance rather than relying on ancestry or strict adherence to laws of purity.[12] The community of the Spirit belongs to the compassionate rule of God dramatically demonstrated in Easter and Pentecost.

Historically, the church has celebrated Pentecost[13] as its birthday. Coming fifty days after Passover, the Feast of Weeks was the time of the harvest and also the commemoration of the giving of the law by Moses. Retaining this continuity with its historical roots is helpful in connecting the cosmopolitan community that congregates in Jerusalem to the historic people of God as well as the nascent church gathered around Jesus. The Israel of God has not been displaced, but "enlarged, opened to outsiders, and thereby wonderfully transformed."[14] Furthermore, Pentecost is not simply a historical event in the first century; it is also an eschatological event in that the vision of a universal experience of Spirit in power comes into view, where "Israel's promise and disciples' wonder converge upon a future present."[15]

Joel's promise (Joel 2:28-32), finally realized, comes in the natural elements long associated with the presence of Spirit—wind, flame, and now the waters of baptism (Acts 2:2-3,41). The stunning display of the Spirit's power evokes skepticism and wonder, scoffing and repentance. After the ascension of the Christ, in Luke's chronology (Luke 24:51; Acts 1:9), the Spirit is poured out on all flesh. When the flesh of Jesus is no longer visible, the community of the Spirit becomes the enfleshment of God. Once again, in vulnerable nearness and humility, God chooses to make a home in the fragility of perishable life. Old and young, male and female, slave and free, Jew and Greek, educated and uneducated—all these are found to be a suitable dwelling by God's Spirit. Indeed, notions of privilege and rank, domination and subordination, insider and outsider, are challenged by the leveling, integrating action of the Spirit. Michael Welker says it well: "When the Spirit of God is poured out, the different persons and groups of people will open God's presence with each other and for each other . . . [and] will make it possible to know the reality intended by God."[16] This reality, a common sharing in the Spirit, stands in stark contrast to the systems of exploitation that arise within structures fabricated by humans. In the Spirit, widely disparate persons will recognize one another as sisters and brothers, friends and family. No one will be able to call another human "unclean," for "God shows no partiality" (Acts 10:15,34). And no one can cling to the world's goods while another is in need.

By the Spirit is born a uniting community characterized by fellowship and ecstasy.[17] This description links the church with the triune life of God, whose relations also are marked by communion and mutual delight, standing outside of self in the giving of life to the others.[18] The Spirit will toil to sustain the *perichoresis* of the varied members of the body of Christ, that they might be one. Delivering this new, redeemed humanity, called from many nations, comes from the long labor of the Spirit of God.

INCORPORATING THROUGH BAPTISM

A significant part of the birthing work of the Spirit is seen in Christian baptism. Ironically, despite having an ecclesial tradition that derives much of its theological identity from the initiating sacrament,[19] contemporary Baptists hold a rather shallow view of baptism. Our spiritual forebears in the Baptist tradition were less concerned about the manner of baptizing than they were about baptizing believers. This was the distinctive over which Anabaptists and Baptists were willing to lay down their lives.[20] These ancestors in faith would have little patience with the later skirmishes fought over the proper mode and the proper administrator of baptism,[21] for these were secondary and tertiary issues for them. Their great concern was for faith to be voluntary, and believer's baptism followed the individual's commitment to following Jesus. Hence, Baptists did not baptize infants, and many churches were reluctant to baptize until late adolescence or early adulthood in order to ensure the personal intentionality of the one being baptized. British Baptists have resisted baptizing younger children, unlike many congregations in America, and are also concerned about loss of meaning of the sacrament in general.[22]

Baptists have rightly pointed to the New Testament basis for the practice of immersion,[23] but this preoccupation has led them to talk too much about water and too little about the Spirit's role in baptism. How are we to think about the distinctive role of the Spirit in the sacrament of baptism? Can we identify the work of the Spirit in the Trinitarian action of incorporation? Is this when the Spirit is given, or at a later time?

Too often, baptism is interpreted in terms of imitation rather than incorporation. Because Jesus was baptized, we should be also, following his example. Even the baptisteries in many of our churches seek to evoke figurations of the Jordan, further extending this identification with Jesus' water baptism. It would be helpful for us to remember the comprehensive character of his baptism, especially since we hope to link our baptism with his through the Spirit. According to the witness of the Gospels, Jesus' baptism is more than what he experienced as he was plunged into the rushing waters of the river at the hand of John, and it is more than his death on the cross, although it is inclusive of both of these events. Jesus' baptism is his whole existence in the form of a servant, all that is included in his being present among humanity "not to be served but to serve" (Mark 10:45). Accepting baptism from John is the beginning of his baptism of vicarious suffering, which could be completed only in the cross. The experience in the Jordan anticipates the dying and rising of Christ, prophetically foreshadowing the extent of his self-giving. He has a baptism yet to undergo (Luke 12:50).

When Jesus poignantly asks his disciples, "Can you be baptized with my baptism?" (Mark 10:38), he is not speaking of a simple initiation rite that could be readily accomplished. Rather, as he speaks of his imminent suffering and death in the language of "being baptized" and "drinking the cup," he is putting before them a specter from which they all will shrink (Matthew 26:56). One cannot imitate fully this baptism; one can only be incorporated into it through the Spirit. Christ's baptism is our baptism by the power of the Spirit, who can bring disparate beings into union.

Paul's baptismal theology complements what we find only in

outline in the Gospels. He had grasped the truth of what the Spirit effects in baptism: the Spirit plunges the believer into the very life of Christ. The Christian does not imitate the baptism of her or his Lord, but is made a participant in it through the power of the Spirit. The Spirit draws believers into the paschal rhythms of Christ. Only in the power of the Spirit can one be baptized with the baptism of Christ; one is crucified with him, yet lives in newness of life. Elizabeth Johnson describes this incorporating movement: Through "the power of the Spirit the beloved community...participates in the living and dying and rising of Christ to such an extent that they can even be called the body of Christ."[24]

The language of the Spirit's role in baptism is striking: "But you were washed, you were sanctified, you were justified in the name of the Lord Jesus Christ and in the Spirit of our God" (1 Corinthians 6:11). The baptismal tradition is summarized here in a doxological and catechetical form: "For in the one Spirit we were all baptized into one body—Jews or Greeks, slaves or free—and we were all made to drink of one Spirit" (1 Corinthians 12:13); explicitly, the Spirit is identified as the agent, even the medium, of baptism into the body of Christ. The role of the Spirit is implied in the statement "As many of you as were baptized into Christ have clothed yourselves with Christ" (Galatians 3:27), as baptism into Christ depends upon the Spirit to unite the believer with Christ. And in the following text, the role of the Spirit links the signs of belonging—circumcision and baptism—to the death and resurrection of Christ: "In him also you were circumcised with a spiritual circumcision, by putting off the body of the flesh in the circumcision of Christ; when you were buried with him in baptism, you were also raised with him through faith in the power of God, who raised him from the dead" (Colossians 2:11-12).

Other New Testament texts suggest the link between baptism and the sacrificial imagery of the death of Jesus: "the exiles...who have been chosen and destined by God the [Creator] and sanctified by the Spirit to be obedient to Jesus Christ and to be sprinkled with his blood" (1 Peter 1:1-2); "how much more will the blood of Christ, who through the eternal Spirit offered himself without blemish to God, purify our conscience from dead works to worship the living God!" (Hebrews 9:14). We see the working of the Spirit with Christ in these texts. Christ's sacrifice, his baptism in blood, is seen as the cleansing agent when the Spirit applies this to those who share in his death. Jesus' baptism, his utter self-giving, becomes our life and death through the power of the Spirit, who unites us with him, as well as all others who receive his baptism with Spirit (Luke 3:16). Christian baptism is baptism in the Spirit (Mark 1:8; John 1:33; Titus 3:5).

On the day I was baptized, I became a member of Christ's body, which carries a deeper and richer connotation than simply being added to the church rolls as one who had conformed to the proper initiation rite. Membership connoted a new relationship to Christ and his body; being baptized into Christ made me a part of the new humanity that God is calling into being, begun in Jesus. By the Spirit, I was united with him and the other members of his body. Organically, there is no relationship to the church apart from relationship to Christ through the Spirit.

The use of the word *body* to mean a group of people is so familiar that we lose its linguistic force. *Corporate*, in fact, now means "social" and nothing else. It is easy, therefore, to forget that this use of the word *body* was quite unfamiliar, if not entirely unknown, to the people to whom Paul was writing. As John Robinson observes, when Paul took the term *sōma* ("body") and applied it to the church, what it conveyed was an idea "not corporate but corporal."[25] It is almost impossible for us to understand fully the organic implications of the Pauline language. Christians form Christ's risen body in the world; by the Spirit they are made one in him.

Where did Paul get such an idea? Many scholars have suggested a Stoic background that spoke of the cosmos in its unity or as a body, or Jewish wisdom thinking, which often reflected upon the idea of corporate personality among a whole people.[26] In my judgment, Paul made this identification based upon his encounter with the risen Christ on the road to Damascus. Paul's perception of the church as the body of Christ is nothing less than an extension of his understanding of incarnation. It is also a direct concomitant of his theology of Spirit. When the risen Christ appeared to him, the "heart of the revelation which came to him was the fact that the Church he was trying to stamp out was no other than Jesus Christ Himself."[27] As Paul recounts, "And I fell to the ground and heard a voice saying to me, 'Saul, Saul, why are you persecuting me?' I answered, 'Who are you, Lord?' Then he said to me, "I am Jesus of Nazareth whom you are persecuting'" (Acts 22:7-8; cf. Acts 26:14-15). This encounter led Paul to understand that the resurrection body of Christ was inclusive of the Christian community.[28]

The community of the Spirit is more than the church as society; it is an embodiment expressing God's merciful nearness. To speak of a society, or even a gathered community (that favorite expression of our Baptist forebears), unfortunately tends in the direction of individualism. Karl Barth articulates the organic model that is grounded in Pauline imagery: "The believers...are therefore, in their full-grown and in no way attenuated individuality, one body, one individual in Christ. They are not a mass of individuals, not even a corporation, a personified society, or a 'totality,' but The Individual, The One, The New...."[29]

What was meant to be a sign of Christian unity often has precipitated schism as believers have overemphasized some aspects of baptism to the neglect of others. While Baptists prize their heritage of dissent, a lingering shadow falls across the tradition of the "believers' church"—the separatist trajectory. In recent years, scholars have become concerned that the legacies of the Enlightenment's stress on the primacy of the individual and of the Baptist voluntary principle have conspired to truncate a robust theology of community in Christ. Baptists have seen themselves joined to a local congregation more than to Christ's body, the new humanity. Their accentuation of congregational autonomy has led to a dismembering of the fullness of incarnation and, hence, a diminished pneumatology. Reclaiming the Spirit's incorporating work in baptism promises a more holistic, organic understanding of the Spirit's embodiment in the church, whose head is Christ.[30]

Now, after all this discussion, we return to the key question with which we began this section: What is the distinctive role of the Spirit in baptism? The Spirit joins the believer to the life of Jesus the Christ; in baptism, the Spirit unites us to the birth, death, and resurrection of the Messiah of God. Our lives are now hidden with Christ in God (Colossians 3:3), and the power that has sustained our whole lives we now recognize as the same power that raised him from the dead. Our lives were not devoid of the Spirit prior to baptism; however, we have not been introduced into the life of Christ himself or experienced the fullness of spiritual power until Christ, our "ark," bears us safely through the deathlike experience that baptism is.[31] We are redeemed from the threat of dying thus by dying and rising with Christ to life born anew.

A sign of this newness and a sign of the unified work of Christ and Holy Spirit is the ancient practice of chrismation—making the sign of the cross with oil on the forehead of the baptized, thereby symbolizing the distinctive presence of Spirit.[32] The connection of anointing with the Spirit is made once again: oil is a "sign of the joy of the Spirit."[33] Although the Spirit is given distinctively in baptism, there are other occasions when the fullness of Spirit is experienced anew. We will explore how the Spirit nourishes at table and enlivens worship in the last two sections of this chapter. There we will see the ongoing birthing work of the Spirit as we learn of our identity within the body of Christ. We turn now to examine the sacrament of Eucharist, a chief means of the Spirit's sustenance in spiritual life.

NOURISHING AT TABLE

We are used to focusing on the presence of the crucified and risen Christ in the time of Communion, as well we should. The meal and the table are commonly referred to as "the Lord's"; he was the founder of this communal expression, and churches to this day celebrate Eucharist in his name.[34] The challenge for us is to consider by what means we meet Christ in this practice of eating and drinking in his name. This requires that we face the ambiguity of something that Calvin described as "in a matter present and in a manner absent."[35] Gathered around the welcoming table, we meet Jesus once again, but there is mystery to this encounter. How is the one who ascended on high present with us, yet absent at the same time? Thus, we must inquire how the Spirit is involved in the representation of Christ in the common sharing of the meal. As in our study of baptism, we have much to explore about the distinctive role of the Holy Spirit in the *synaxis* (union), the community gathered for Christ's feast with the church.[36]

While not all the resurrection appearances of Jesus occur during a meal, considerable linkage exists between the common meal and the recognition of the risen Christ (Mark 16:14-18; Luke 24:13-53; John 21; Acts 1:4-5). Probably the most directly eucharistic of the appearances is that at the shared meal at Emmaus, told by Luke. Luke's richly textured narrative, beloved by preachers and hearers alike, recounts an experience of wonder as hearts burn and eyes open to the Christ in their midst. The fire of the Spirit kindles their recognition of divine presence, drawing them to Jesus, reminiscent of the fire of the unconsumed bush drawing Moses into the presence of God (Exodus 3:2-3), who is Spirit. Opening the eyes of the blind is also characteristic of the Spirit-empowered time of the messiah.

Accordingly, the Spirit awakens the two travelers to the presence of Jesus in the breaking of the bread, and then he vanishes (Luke 24:30-31). Michael Welker offers a perceptive insight about this sequence: "Recognition of the risen Christ by means of the senses and the withdrawal of the risen Christ belong together."[37] His interpretation suggests that it is only by the Spirit that persons can recognize the presence of Christ; the usual methods of rational cognition and sensory experience will not suffice when seeking to engage the One who cannot be contained in life or in death. In light of this disassociation of resurrection appearance from tangible phenomena, connecting the presence of Jesus directly with the elements of the meal seems unwarranted.[38] And yet, our experience in Communion is like that of those who journeyed to Emmaus; it was in the concrete experience of eating that they recognized him who had made table fellowship the centerpiece of his ministry.[39] The sustained eucharistic practice of the church argues inexorably for linking the complex event of eating the bread and drinking the cup with the ongoing presence of Jesus Christ through the Spirit.

Reflecting on the experience of the baptized at the meal, Yves Congar writes, "Jesus is in us, but, if his sacramental presence is to have its effect, the Holy Spirit must add his breath, his fire and his dynamism."[40] Surely, we affirm that when we gather at the Lord's Table, Christ is within each individual, but even more importantly, we affirm that Christ is in our collective midst, and we all are one in him. The breath and fire and dynamic power of the Spirit provide the means of encountering Jesus and one another. It is the Spirit who re-members the baptized as the body of Christ.

One day in chapel at the seminary where I teach, this became graphically clear to me. The student leader[41] had the imaginative insight that if we did Communion in reverse, we might understand better that we really are a part of one another and of Christ. As we entered the sacred space, each person was given a small cup of juice and a portion of the loaf. We juggled these elements a bit uneasily through the hymns and prayers, feeling a bit awkward. Then the transforming event occurred. We were invited to the table to make whole and make one Christ's presence in the meal. As each of us poured our little vessel back into the large chalice and placed our morsel of bread on the paten, we understood afresh how together we participate in God, joined by the Spirit in Christ. Each communicant mattered, and our unity was demonstrated. We recognized Christ as we recognized one another, and the body was re-membered. That day, the words of Paul were enacted in our worship: "The cup of blessing that we bless, is it not a sharing in the blood of Christ? The bread that we break, is it not a sharing in the body of Christ? Because there is one bread, we who are many are one body, for we all partake of the one bread" (1 Corinthians 10:16-17).

Baptists have focused mainly on *anamnesis*—remembering Jesus in a memorial meal—following the instruction of 1 Corinthians 11:23-26. We have thought of this remembrance as a cognitive activity of bringing to memory Christ's death for us. The draping of the table often has connoted a funereal image: his body is laid out before the congregation, whose chief action in the meal is to be somber.

Laurence Hull Stookey reminds us that there is a lot more to remembering: it is not mental recall, but doing the meal. We take bread and wine, give thanks, break the loaf, and share the cup and the bread with all gathered.[42] In the meal we participate in the most fundamental human act: we eat, receiving from the hands of one another what God provides through the labor of Spirit-empowered humans, of whom Jesus is "first" among many sisters and brothers (1 Corinthians 15:23). Our eating makes us present to one another as Christ hosts us. We give thanks for the founding meal, all the meals we share, and that great meal yet to come, "when Christ himself will serve us, with sweet manna all around." This anticipatory aspect of Communion is all but lost "where the church has come to feel at home in the world," observes William Cavanaugh.[43]

At times, we conduct the meal as if all the meaning depends upon our right action in how we prepare and serve and receive the elements. But our actions cannot make the practice a means of grace; rather, we live into the reality of the self-giving of God embodied in the feast spread before us.

The table itself communicates welcome and hospitality.[44] The table symbolizes justice, equality, and embodiedness. When celebrating the meal in an African American Baptist congregation, it is common for ministers to ask, "Has everyone been served?" prior to partaking. What a wonderful expression of hospitality! Table fellowship is not meant to exclude, but to nourish. And what is more nourishing than for those presiding to make sure that all have been served, that their presence has been honored?

The pastoral question also reminds us that Christ's table calls us to justice. How can we be thankful for the fullness on this table and yet ignore the emptiness on so many other tables? How can we celebrate our unity in Christ at this table, yet refuse to welcome those "others" to put their feet under the tables in our homes? We must see the connection between the eucharistic meal and all those other meals, where often we belie our theology of Communion by our exclusionary table manners.

One reason that those traditions which stress the symbolic over the sacramental aspects of the meal do not think of the Communion meal as particularly nourishing is that they have not identified their true hunger. Eucharist is about helping us know what we hunger for, the true bread that can satisfy. John's version of the institution of the eucharistic meal (John 6:24-34), couched in the story of the wilderness feeding, presses us to consider our real hunger, the "hunger behind and beneath all other hungers,"[45] in the words of Fred Craddock. Hunger, then, is not just about food.

The clamoring crowd from Capernaum wanted Jesus to outdo Moses. Popular belief looked for a recurrence of manna in the messianic age, according to 2 Baruch. It appears that those pressing in on Jesus wanted little more than this. But Jesus wanted their inquiry to focus on the food that lasts, "the food that endures for eternal life" (John 6:27). Earlier in the Fourth Gospel, he spoke of living water that will quench one's deepest thirst (John 4:7-14), an image of the Spirit; now he speaks of bread, meaning his life broken for them.

It is not surprising that they and we do not really know what we hunger for—our market-driven culture weaves a web of seduction. "Consume" is the categorical imperative of our day; meaning has been reduced to the economy. And we buy and eat, and eat and buy…and still we hunger. It is never enough, for it is perishable bread. Only the bread of life, Jesus, can fill us as we commune with him in the meal. Stookey sums up the agency of the Spirit in nourishing Christians: "It is by the power of the Spirit that bread and wine can mean more than gustatory pleasure and physiological nutrition, that these ordinary table items can be the body and blood of Christ—Christ incarnate, crucified, risen, present in the world, and reigning in righteousness."[46] The Spirit helps us discern our true hunger and nourishes us in the common meal, where Christ always meets us. We hunger for belonging, a place of welcome.[47] We hunger for intimacy, to offer ourselves to someone who will receive us, who will know us to our depths and delight in us. These things Christ does, through our brothers and sisters who are brought into union through the Spirit.

This short study does not allow us to trace the varied perspectives that have tended to demarcate ecclesial traditions. It appears that pluralism in eucharistic practices has existed from the time of the New Testament and the early church.[48] For example, the mode of Christ's presence in the supper has long been a matter of great curiosity. Chloe Breyer offers a wonderful example of the mysterious association of the divine presence with the quotidian elements of wine and bread. She recounts an experience from her internship at the Cathedral of St. John the Divine in Harlem when a children's worker, Gina, attempted to explain to children what happens in the experience of Communion.

> "Look at this thing!" Gina says, pointing to the wafer. "Look at how small and thin it is. How could God, who is everywhere all the time, all over the universe, possibly fit inside this little piece of food? I mean, really! How could this happen?"

Gina goes on to describe what the priest is doing when consecrating the bread.

> "So when the priest is standing up there behind the altar holding this little wafer above her head, what is she doing?" Gina continues, still holding the wafer aloft. "The priest is asking, 'Please, God, will you get in here? Will you just come and get in here, please! We know you can do everything, God, so will you please just come here and be in this wafer now!'"[49]

Baptists emphasize Christ's presence in the community rather than in the elements; however, following Calvin, they do believe that Christ is especially in attendance at the celebration of the meal as spiritual presence. Thus, the prayers are not for God to "get in" the bread and the cup, but for communicants to recognize Jesus in their midst by the power of the Spirit. Historically, the prayer known as the epiclesis (meaning "to call upon") is for the Spirit to suffuse the meal with divine power. The epiclesis calls upon God to send the Holy Spirit upon the bread and wine, suggesting that the work of transformation is to occur in the elements. Baptists can helpfully appropriate this traditional prayer by inviting the Spirit to transform the congregation into a vital expression of the body of Christ. Hence, the epiclesis is not about transformation of the elements, but of the communicants.[50] This the Spirit continually does, and in the next chapter we will consider the metamorphosis of glory that goes on in the lives of Christians.

As in the midwifery of baptism, it is the Spirit's movement in the meal that makes the sacrament effectual, making all the participants present to one another. "Eucharistic presence" refers to Christ and his body, to whom we are joined in the Spirit. As central acts of Christian liturgy, baptism and the shared meal form us into the new identity birthed in the Spirit. In the final section of this chapter, we now consider other ways in which the Spirit enlivens the worship of the church.

ENLIVENING IN WORSHIP

We all know that there are times in worship when we are deeply moved. We describe this as "feeling the Spirit," or as African Americans often put it, "We had church today." When this occurs, the faithful have a sense that something beyond our planning or control happened in that sacred time and place. Somehow we were caught up together in a movement of God that provoked wonder, ecstasy, and expressions of service. Our songs soar, our prayers take flight, and our hearts are lifted up to God. We experience the holy as well as the human as God serves us and we give ourselves to God and one another anew.

We also know that there are times when we attend worship out of habit or obligation, often lacking any expectation that we will be met by the Holy Spirit. Our souls are parched, and we long for living water but doubt the supply of the Spirit in the aridity of our efforts. Don Saliers pointedly asks, "Why do we settle for so little when God offers so much in Word, sacrament, and song?"[51] I suggest that our negligible attention to pneumatology is partly to blame. It is the Spirit who calls the thirsty to the well of worship. It is the Spirit who creates the hunger for communion with God and others. It is the Spirit who makes us present to one another, receptive and welcoming. It is the Spirit who prompts voices too long silent to speak.[52] It is the Spirit who "delivers us from a narcissistic preoccupation with the self to find our true being in loving communion with God and one another," as James Torrance observes.[53]

The very notion of gathering for worship, assembling as those who bear the name of Christ, is a Spirit-crafted venture. The early chapters of Acts chronicle all kinds of church meetings! The first believers were together almost constantly—in the temple, in the streets, in their homes. As a growing body of believers, they understood the strengthening that came from sharing their lives with one another. Their baptism in the fire of Spirit kindled a new gladness and generosity (Acts 2:44-47).

Coming together as resurrection people on the first day of the week was driven by the wind of the Spirit. We must consider, consequently, what it means to be "in the Spirit on the Lord's Day" (Revelation 1:10), as the seer of the Apocalypse describes his experience. Furthermore, what are some of the specific ways in which the Spirit enlivens the community's worship, enabling the dance of joy? We now address the Spirit's role in prayer and in song.

Rather than being a movement between God and humanity, prayer can become an exercise in legalism whereby one thinks that if she or he "gets it right," God is compelled to respond. But the language of prayer is often too deep for words, and formulaic precision eludes us. Sighs, groans, and the fathomless murmurings of troubled spirits are understood by God's inward presence. The truth of our fragmented lives cannot be spoken in crisp coherence; we must rely on the One who "searches everything, even the depths of God" (1 Corinthians 2:10). Only the Spirit understands the incoherence of suffering. According to Paul, that great theologian of prayer, we have the assurance that the Spirit gathers up the prayer of the church and conveys it to God: "Likewise the Spirit helps us in our weakness; for we do not know how to pray as we ought, but that very Spirit intercedes with sighs too deep for words. And God, who searches the heart, knows what is the mind of the Spirit, because the Spirit intercedes for the saints according to the will of God" (Romans 8:26-27). Prayer as "shared life with God"—Roberta Bondi's winsome definition[54]—depends on the connection that the Spirit establishes between divine and human life. We pray because we are beckoned to do so in the power of the Spirit; "true prayer begins with God," as one of my theology professors loved to say.[55]

When praying in the Spirit, one remains a unique individual, with her or his own particular needs, yet is a part of the larger prayer of the church. The movements of thanksgiving, confession, intercession, and supplication weave the concerns of each with the concerns of all. The breathing of the Spirit inspires those who pray and stirs them to recognize the response of God, whose life we share. It is only by the sustaining breath of the Spirit that we can pray "at all times" (Ephesians 6:18) and "without ceasing" (1 Thessalonians 5:17).

The epigram attributed to St. Augustine, "Whoever sings [to God, in worship], prays twice,"[56] articulates the significant interface between prayer and song as Spirit-inspired liturgical actions.

Ruach sustains song—indeed, insists on song.[57] Singing is one of the most embodied aspects of our worship. Our very bodies become instruments for praise or lament as breath and word create an offering to God. Again and again we are enjoined to sing our faith in the community of the Spirit: "Be filled with the Spirit, as you sing psalms and hymns and spiritual songs among yourselves, singing and making melody to the Lord in your hearts" (Ephesians 5:18-19); "With gratitude in your hearts sing psalms, hymns, and spiritual songs to God" (Colossians 3:16). We learn our faith through singing it; somehow we learn it better when it is set to moving rhythm and lyrical tune. Besides, how can we join the dance with the Spirit if we cannot hear the music?

Communal singing is fading away in our culture. Church and ball games are about the only places where it is regularly practiced.[58] Song as integral to the worship of the church must not be diminished by being handed over to the experts, the performers, or the electronic. When we sing together, we embody the unity and harmony (hopefully!) of the body of Christ, empowered by Holy Breath. Singing is profoundly vulnerable, yet hopeful; lifting voice to God amidst all the currents of life demonstrates a profound participation in the cadences of God.

When sharing in the *opus Dei* (prayer as the work of God) in Benedictine communities, I am always amazed at how many of the monks know most of the Psalter by heart. They may glance at their service books on occasion, but the seasoned ones have psalms and chants so wedded to their beings that "praying twice" is as natural as breathing for them. Prayer through song has given faith stability and direction, and it has regularly provided joy and beauty, lovely graces of the Spirit of God.

In this chapter we have focused primarily on the corporate expressions of the Spirit's labor. The Spirit's birthing and transforming work continues, however, in the lives of individual persons, forming them after the likeness of Christ.

NOTES

1. In her *Discipleship of Equals: A Critical Feminist Ekklesia-logy of Liberation* (New York: Crossroad, 1993), Schüssler Fiorenza extends the argument that she put forward in *In Memory of Her: A Feminist Reconstruction of Christian Origins* (New York: Crossroad, 1983).

2. This is Geiko Müller-Fahrenholz's memorable description in *God's Spirit: Transforming a World in Crisis* (New York: Continuum, 1995), 37.

3. Thomas N. Finger sees the need for much contemporary work to be done in ecclesiology, as it "has often been one of theology's least innovative and interesting loci" (*Christian Theology: An Eschatological Approach*, vol. 2 [Scottdale, Pa.: Herald Press, 1989], 225–226). I agree that fresh inquiry is needed in this area.

4. Paul D. Hanson has written perhaps the most comprehensive treatment of this biblical theme, *The People Called: The Growth of Community in the Bible* (Louisville: Westminster John Knox, 2001).

5. Many feminist scholars have examined the ways in which Jesus did not conform to traditional rabbinic reserve in relating to women. Lisa Isherwood summarizes and updates the works of others writing in the field of feminist Christology in *Introducing Feminist Christologies* (Cleveland: Pilgrim Press, 2002).

6. See, for example, John H. Elliot, *A Home for the Homeless: A Sociological Exegesis of 1 Peter, Its Situation and Strategy*, rev. ed. (Minneapolis: Fortress, 1990); Jerome H. Neyrey, ed., *The Social World of Luke–Acts: Models for Interpretation* (Peabody, Mass.: Hendrickson, 1991).

7. Bruce Malina, *The Social Gospel of Jesus: The Kingdom of God in Mediterranean Perspective* (Minneapolis: Fortress, 2001), 34.

8. Hanson, *The People Called*, 391. Hanson's comment may be less than fair to many contemporary monastics whose social advocacy is unparalleled.

9. Malina, *Social Gospel of Jesus*, 68.

10. Richard A. Horsley and Neil Asher Silberman, commenting upon the healings offered to non-Israelites (Mark 7:24-30; Matthew 8:5-13), suggest that Jesus may have "originally envisioned an outreach to all the world's people" (*The Message and the Kingdom: How Jesus and Paul Ignited a Revolution and Transformed the Ancient World* [Minneapolis: Fortress, 1997], 117).

11. Hanson, *The People Called*, 392.

12. Ibid.

13. Pentecost literally means "fiftieth day," which was the Greek term given to the Jewish Feast of Weeks.

14. James W. McClendon Jr., *Systematic Theology: Doctrine*, vol. 2 (Nashville: Abingdon, 1994), 363.

15. Ibid., 310.

16. Michael Welker, *God the Spirit*, trans. John F. Hoffmeyer (Minneapolis: Fortress, 1994), 151.

17. These are two of McClendon's choice words for describing Christian community.

18. Miroslav Volf links Trinity to ecclesiology in a constructive proposal for a Protestant vision of church *vis-à-vis* Catholic and Orthodox models (*After Our Likeness: The Church as the Image of the Trinity* [Grand Rapids: Eerdmans, 1998]).

19. I am aware that today most Baptists do not use the language of sacrament; however, their English Baptist forebears had no hesitance in using this terminology. I use it intentionally in my writing and teaching in order to help contemporary Baptists recover some of the depth of meaning lost in our observance of baptism and Communion.

20. See Robert G. Torbet, *A History of the Baptists*, 3rd ed. (Valley Forge, Pa.: Judson Press, 1973), 516–517.

21. See Dale Moody, *Baptism: Foundation for Christian Unity* (Philadelphia: Westminster, 1967), 240-252; see also George R. Beasley-Murray, *Baptism in the New Testament* (London: Paternoster, 1962).

22. Paul S. Fiddes and others are seeking to address this diminished baptismal theology through a collection of essays entitled *Reflections on the Water: Understanding God and the World through the Baptism of Believers* (Macon, Ga.: Smyth and Helwys, 1996).

23. See R. Wayne Stacy, "Baptism," in *A Baptist's Theology*, ed. R. Wayne Stacy (Macon, Ga.: Smyth and Helwys, 1999), 152–174.

24. Elizabeth A. Johnson, *She Who Is: The Mystery of God in Feminist Theological Discourse* (New York: Crossroad, 1992), 72.

25. John A. T. Robinson, *The Body: A Study in Pauline Theology* (Philadelphia: Westminster, 1952), 50.

26. To explore the background of this imagery further, see W. D. Davies, *Paul and Rabbinic Judaism*, 4th ed. (Philadelphia: Fortress, 1980), 36–50.

27. Robinson, *The Body*, 58.

28. Ibid.

29. Karl Barth, *The Epistle to the Romans*, trans. Edwyn C. Hoskyns (Oxford: Oxford University Press, 1933), 443.

30. See Molly T. Marshall, "The Fullness of Incarnation: God's New Humanity in the Body of Christ," *Review and Expositor* 93, no. 2 (spring 1996): 187–201.

31. The Petrine catechesis uses flood imagery to instruct about baptism (1 Peter 3:18-22).

32. See the helpful discussion on the variations of this practice in Laurence Hull Stookey, *Baptism: Christ's Act in the Church* (Nashville: Abingdon, 1982), 109–115. The separation between baptism and confirmation is fraught with problems and creates confusion about when the Spirit is given. See Yves Congar, *I Believe in the Holy Spirit*, vol. 3, trans. David Smith (New York: Crossroad,

1997), 218–220.

33. Stookey, *Baptism*, 109.

34. For a comprehensive survey of the biblical grounding for eucharistic practice, see Eugene LaVerdiere, *The Eucharist in the New Testament and the Early Church* (Collegeville, Minn.: Liturgical Press, 1996). For a systematic perspective, see Michael Welker, *What Happens in Holy Communion?* trans. John F. Hoffmeyer (Grand Rapids: Eerdmans, 2000). In the churches of my youth, Eucharist invariably was referred to as the "Lord's Supper," probably following the Southern custom of calling the evening meal "supper" and our practice of celebrating it in the evening service.

35. Cited in Douglas Farrow, *Ascension and Ecclesia: On the Significance of the Doctrine of the Ascension for Ecclesiology and Christian Cosmology* (Grand Rapids: Eerdmans, 1999), 3.

36. I owe this description to Laurence Hull Stookey, from the title of his excellent book *Eucharist: Christ's Feast with the Church* (Nashville: Abingdon, 1993).

37. Welker, *What Happens in Holy Communion?* 14.

38. The history of the perspective known as "consubstantiation" (presently a debated term among Lutherans), where Christ's presence is somehow linked to the elements themselves, is much too complex to take up here. See the discussion by Stookey, *Eucharist*, 180–181.

39. Dennis E. Smith and Hal E. Taussig describe the meals in the Jesus movement as "slanderously open to outsiders" (*Many Tables: The Eucharist in the New Testament and Liturgy Today* [Philadelphia: Trinity Press International, 1990], 50).

40. Congar, *I Believe*, 264.

41. The student was Rev. Nicole Finkelstein-Blair, a 2001 graduate of Central Baptist Theological Seminary, who kindly gave her permission to share this story here.

42. See Stookey, *Eucharist*, 28–29.

43. William T. Cavanaugh, *Torture and Eucharist: Theology, Politics, and the Body of Christ* (Oxford: Blackwell, 1998), 225.

44. Letty Russell has offered considerable reflection on the meaning of table for the community gathered in the name of Jesus. See her *Church in the Round: Feminist Interpretation of the Church* (Louisville: Westminster John Knox, 1993).

45. Fred B. Craddock, *John* (Atlanta: John Knox, 1982), 53.

46. Stookey, *Eucharist*, 100.

47. June Christian Goudey suggests that one of the factors contributing to the erosion of eucharistic practice is the vision of God as the dominating one who demands the death of "his" Son (*The Feast of Our Lives: Re-imaging Communion* [Cleveland: Pilgrim Press, 2002], 22–26).

48. LaVerdiere, *The Eucharist*, 185.

49. Chloe Breyer, *The Close: A Young Woman's First Year at Seminary* (New York: Basic Books, 2000), 168–69.

50. Fr. Wilfred Theisen, a Benedictine monk of St. John's Abbey, teased about the doctrine of transubstantiation, saying that it takes no more faith to believe that the elements on the table could literally be the body of Christ than to believe that this bread, which he disdainfully called "fish food," could be real bread! Ah, theological dialogue at its finest!

51. Don E. Saliers, *Worship Come to Its Senses* (Nashville: Abingdon, 1996), 15.

52. Janet Wootton speaks of women "whispering the liturgy" because of exclusive words and practices employed in worship (*Introducing a Practical Feminist Theology of Worship* [Cleveland: Pilgrim Press, 2000], 17–33).

53. James B. Torrance, *Worship, Community and the Triune God of Grace* (Downers Grove, Ill.: InterVarsity, 1996), 41.

54. See Roberta Bondi, *To Pray and To Love: Conversations on Prayer with the Early Church* (Minneapolis: Fortress, 1991).

55. I learned the phrase from Dr. Wayne E. Ward, longtime professor at Southern Baptist Theological Seminary, Louisville, Kentucky.

56. As cited in Brian Wren, *Praying Twice: The Music and Words of Congregational Song* (Louisville: Westminster John Knox, 2000), 1.

57. Don E. Saliers, "Singing Our Lives," in *Practicing Our Faith: A Way of Life for a Searching People*, ed. Dorothy C. Bass (San Francisco: Jossey-Bass, 1997), 180.

58. Ibid., 192.

CHAPTER 6

TRANSFORMING UNFINISHED PRESENCE

*And all of us, with unveiled faces, seeing the glory
of the Lord as though reflected in a mirror,
are being transformed into the same image from
one degree of glory to another; for this
comes from the Lord, the Spirit.*
—2 Corinthians 3:18

WE HAVE SPOKEN OF THE SPIRIT AS THE BREATH OF ALL LIFE; THIS
insight leads us to a new valuing of all creation and a new respect
for the spiritual longings of all humanity. In this chapter[1] we turn
to a question more familiar to many of us: How do human beings
open themselves to the work of the Spirit in order to become most
fully personal? Or, asked from the other direction: What is the role
of the Spirit in forming us into living icons of God? And then,
what do our receptivity and praxis mean for the unfolding of the
divine life? These hard questions lead us into a discussion of spiritual formation as a synergism of the Spirit and attentive humans.[2]

What is spiritual formation? Perhaps I should begin by saying
what it is not: it is not a separable part of life, a sort of disembod-
ied denial of the full range of human experience. We do not have
to flee the world or deny our humanity in order to embark on our
life's project of spiritual formation. This world and all our relationships in it are potential sculptors of God's formative work in
our lives. Christian leaders, however, have not always known this.

In the eleventh century, the Byzantine emperor Constantine IX,
judging females too great a threat to spiritual life, signed a char-
ter barring them from crossing the boundaries of Mount Athos,

an enclave dotted with twenty monasteries. Even the donkeys that serve as the only mode of transportation on the steep, rocky slopes of this Aegean peninsula must be males. Thus, no woman had ever seen Mount Athos's priceless treasures—until recently. Women still cannot come to the monasteries, but the site's fabled riches are being allowed to leave. Their destination is the new Byzantine Museum of nearby Thessaloniki; the exhibit opened on June 21, 1997. For the first time, women are able to see 621 unique objects of church art. The decision is being hailed as a sign of the elders' new self-confidence. The outside world no longer seems so menacing.[3] This amusing turn of events suggests that even Greek monasteries are growing in their willingness to "go public" with their spirituality. And so should we.

The contemporary discussion of spirituality is fraught with competing claims. Until about a decade ago, most persons in the Free Church tradition knew very little about spiritual formation. (Some probably thought that it was early morning exercise at camp to ensure "firm believers," or that it was walking in a straight line to required chapel at a Christian college.) Formation was thought to be an exclusively Catholic term, a regimented preparation for those with a vocation to religious life. It entailed adopting a rule, a careful methodical approach to spiritual disciplines, which shaped the whole life of the novice or seminarian. Today in the Free Church context, attending to one's spiritual formation is considered as important as learning biblical exegesis, homiletical skills, theological and liturgical history, and pastoral care.

Protestants are awakening to the significance of a practice-based spirituality, as the writings of Dorothy Bass[4] and Robert Wuthnow[5] suggest. Why has it taken so long? A theological legacy is at work here. The Protestant Reformation's insistence on *sola fide* (faith alone) has, unfortunately, fostered a deep suspicion about the efficacy of any human effort in matters of salvation. "Only believe" became the watchword for those shaped by a tradition that accented the justifying action of God to the neglect of "growing in grace," the transforming movement of sanctification.[6] In addition, hyper-Calvinist strands within the Reformed and Baptist traditions have distorted the biblical idea of perseverance and treated it as a logical corollary of God's unilateral election; therefore, the Pauline exhortation "Work out your own salvation with fear and trembling" (Philippians 2:12) has been muted, or even silenced. Contemporary Baptists need to reclaim perseverance as an essential expression of personal redemption. The Wesleyan tradition has been much healthier, emphasizing the labor of the Christian toward "perfection." In Wesley's view, it is the "diligent believer's responsibility to spare no effort in tapping into the Holy Spirit's sanctifying work."[7]

Alongside this theological legacy is our acquisitive culture's preoccupation with achievement, programmed outcomes, and easily won certitude. Give us the formula, the expert opinion, or the right software, and we are certain we can solve the problem. The acute spiritual longing of contemporary persons—what Mark Burrows calls "soul hunger"[8]—makes us vulnerable to purveyors of quick-fix spiritual antidotes to the unfathomable emptiness that characterizes the spiritual lives of many, even among those who claim Christian identity. Patient, receptive, collaborative process with the divine Spirit, in which one's true spiritual identity is forged over time, seems strangely out of sync with today's instant communication, instant credit, and instant gratification.

Attentiveness to the interior life, long the staple of monastic life, is gaining ground among Protestant ecclesial communions. Retreat houses are full; spiritual directors are in demand; academies of spiritual formation are flourishing; even seminaries like the one where I teach are designing curricula with new emphasis upon what students are becoming, not just what they are learning. The spiritual geography of a theological education now follows the contours of the whole life of persons being formed for ministry.

The cynical refrain "Keep it in the cloister; it won't work in the demands of real life" is being drowned out by a new appreciation for ancient forms of spiritual discipline and community throughout our culture. Appropriating these practices, contemporary Christians and other seekers are experiencing a new sense of transcendence and divine companionship in their daily living. Indeed, the divide between intellectual inquiry and the devotional life, which Thomas Aquinas fostered, is finally being bridged in our day.[9]

How does God's work of transformation occur in our lives? I propose a theology of spiritual formation as "unfinished presence." As John's first epistle puts it, "What we will be has not yet been revealed" (1 John 3:2); however, we have traces, inchoate longings, the welling up of hope, all of which are crafting our grace-full participation in the very life of God. What is the goal of human living as Christians and how are we to move toward this destiny to which God beckons us? How will we become most fully God's and most fully ourselves? These are not antithetical pursuits; as Colin Gunton argues, the Spirit, "far from abolishing, rather maintains and even strengthens particularity. It is not a spirit of merging or assimilation—of homogenization— but of relation in otherness, relation which does not subvert but establishes the other in its true reality."[10] The Spirit is closer than our very breath; more knowledgeable of our unique identities than we are ourselves is our divine companion who "searches everything, even the depths of God" (1 Corinthians 2:10).

Venturing with the Spirit into lifelong transformation is a daunting task. As Margaret Miles observes, "In the entertainment culture of contemporary North America, there are few cultural inducements to understand one's life as an integrated project."[11] And yet, that is precisely our calling if we are Christians: to view the whole of our lives through the paschal rhythms of salvation, that we might, as Paul says, "make our own that for which Christ has made us his own" (Philippians 3:12). Transformation is painstakingly slow, yet we are assisted at every turn.

Second Corinthians 3:18, with its image of pneumatic transformation or metamorphosis of glory, is the backdrop to my development of the idea of "unfinished presence" in these movements: (1) unveiling our faces; (2) transfiguring divine presence; (3) changing from glory into glory; and (4) seeing face to face. Real presence comes about through an abiding communion of persons, divine and human. Christian spirituality bears the marks of unfinished presence throughout our pilgrimage toward what spiritual teachers have called the "beatific vision," when we shall see the Christ "as he is" (1 John 3:2) by the power of the abiding Spirit. Dare we say that divine presence is unfinished as well? What does God's inclusion of humanity in the divine perichoretic movement mean for the fullness of divine presence? Necessarily, our pneumatological reflection will now be more directly related to Christology; however, the Spirit will not be subordinated as if only an agent of Christ—it is a much more reciprocal, perichoretic relationship.

UNVEILING OUR FACES

We are meant for closer relationship to God than has been evident throughout human history. Our forebears turned away from the One who desired to walk and talk in the garden at the time of the evening breeze, as Genesis 3:8 describes the original divine-human intimacy. Not content to be those in whom God delighted, they had the inordinate desire to be as God, "knowing good from evil." Certainly God wanted this too, but as a gift, not as something to be grasped.[12] Adam and Eve gazed longingly at what was forbidden, just out of reach, rather than toward the One whom they were created to image. They sought to establish their own presence independent of the One who formed them.

Presence is a relational concept; we know our personhood through relating to others, even though "otherness" remains a difficult challenge for humans who tend to be *incurvatum in se* (curved in upon oneself).[13] Our identity is established by communing with others, even as the divine persons draw identity through perichoretic movement.

Scripture correlates Spirit, presence, and face. God's Spirit is the mode of God's presence; when God's face is hidden, persons cannot experience the divine presence (*panim*). Psalm 139:7 illustrates this correlation: "Where can I go from your spirit [*ruach*]? Or where can I flee from your presence [*panim*]?" A similar sense appears in Psalm 104:29: "When you hide your face [*panim*], they are dismayed; when you take away their [your?] breath [*ruach*], they die and return to their dust." The connection between face, presence, and Spirit is seen even more clearly in Psalm 51:11, where "your holy spirit" (*ruach*) is rendered as an equivalent parallel to "your presence" (*panim*): "Do not cast me away from your presence, and do not take your holy spirit from me."[14] Paul draws Spirit, face, and presence together in a remarkable way in 2 Corinthians 3:18, depicting the perichoretic movement between humans and God.

Created to love God and to reflect the divine presence, humans early on exercised a propensity to love the creation more than the Creator. Long ago, St. Augustine wrote (in the noninclusive language of his time), "For when there is a question as to whether a man is good, one does not ask what he believes, or what he hopes, but what he loves."[15] Our love, like that of our ancestors, often is misdirected. We confuse means and ends: some things are to be used and others are to be enjoyed. Our problem as humans is that we tend to use God for some greater good, when, in fact, God is only to be enjoyed (according to St. Augustine). We, like our human forebears, are described as being those who "fall short of the glory of God" (Romans 3:23). As a child, I used to ponder this text. Of course, I reasoned, we all fall short of God's glory because we are not God. Only later in theological study did I learn that to fall short is to refuse to reflect the presence—that is, the glory—of God. Remarkably, a distinctive way that Scripture speaks of glory is the human representation of the divine. We are the glory of God! Thus, falling short of God's glory is our refusal to turn toward the divine; not only do we fail to image the holy, but also we refuse to claim our true identity. St. Irenaeus said it best: "The glory of God is humanity fully alive!"

The mysterious and graphic contrast of the modes of God's presence makes it difficult for humans to see clearly. Blaise Pascal understood the paradox of presence in absence, which permeates the entire Bible: "A religion which does not affirm that God is hidden is not true."[16] God comes in the grandeur of the heights of Sinai and in the disfigured, suffering Servant, from whom we hide our faces (Isaiah 53:3). The elusive reconfiguring of divinity throughout Scripture[17] makes human encounter with the Holy One risky, even dangerous. Walter Brueggemann observes that the recurring theme of God's face, present but hidden, shows Israel's ambivalence about knowing by "seeing."[18]

Humanity's fear of the divine presence leaves the face veiled, and thus the divine image often is unrecognizable or nearly effaced. The incident revisited in 2 Corinthians 3:18 is well known. Moses ascended the mountain to receive the law from the Holy One, and the encounter transformed his visage so that his face shone with the reflected glory of God. Although it was but a reflection of God's glory on Moses' face, all who saw him knew that he had been in the presence of the Living God. Yet even this was too much for those fearful of the expression of God's splendor. Paul recontextualizes this understanding when he speaks of the permanent transformation that comes to those who unveil fear and suspicion of God's trustworthiness and look steadily toward the glory of the Lord.

How is this fearless beholding possible? Can one look upon God and live (Exodus 33:20)? Only if God draws back the veil on the divine face. Are we prepared for what might occur when we encounter the Holy One in our likeness? In the words of Stephanie Paulsell, "There is an intimate connection between sacredness and vulnerability."[19] God's transfiguration into the form of humanity, conceived by the Spirit, calls us to transfigure our lives too.

TRANSFIGURING THE DIVINE PRESENCE

Is my presumption that the Spirit of God is present in our world, actively seeking to transform those who open themselves to pneumatic work, justified? Many postmodern interpreters decry what they see as a naïve belief in the presence of any universal power. "The dominant experience of postmodernism is the absence of such presence."[20] As Mark Taylor puts it, "Absolute plenitude and total presence are nowhere to be found."[21] Scripture and theology are actually more modest in their claims about the availability of divine presence than the postmodern critique supposes. Yet its skepticism prompts humility: we should not claim too much. We must not accent the "unfinished presence" of the human in a way incommensurate with unfinished divine presence. Indeed, it is the interplay between the two that brings about seeing face to face.

Hebrew Scripture is forthright in its proscription of graven images to represent God; furthermore, humans cannot presume to encounter the divine visage. Indeed, Moses could see only God's back after requesting to "see God,"[22] which prompted Martin Luther to comment at length on the "hind parts of God."[23] (How's that for a sermon series topic! Some occasions just seem to call for Luther's earthy exegesis.) Annie Dillard is perturbed by God's hiddenness, and she writes of this biblical episode,

"Just a glimpse, Moses: a cleft in the rock here, a mountaintop there, and the rest is denial and longing. You have to stalk everything."[24] Surely, this often is our experience, "stalking God," longing for a glimpse. Exodus 33 is the "most sustained and delicate attempt to deal with the problem of Yahweh's presence/absence in Israel."[25] God's reticence about revealing the divine face has to do with sustaining sovereign freedom; however, God will sustain the commitment to be with Moses. It seems that God does not want the certitude of "seeing" to replace the trust demanded by "not seeing."[26] Yet, the same chapter also has an account of a more intimate encounter, when Moses and God converse as "friend to friend." The juxtaposition of texts such as these underscores the elusiveness of presence. God's definitive befriending of humanity, however, awaits the coming of Christ and the universal experience of the Spirit.

The Spirit of God, in humility and grace, offers a human face in Jesus.[27] In him, God enters the turmoil and promise of the human trajectory and bends it toward the possibility of union with God's own life. This union will not diminish individuality, Christianity maintains, but ultimately enhance it. Once the individual is joined to the depth of God through baptism and the transforming work of the Holy Spirit, that person begins to become a self, is freed to shake off masks and shed false identities, and to become authentic—like Jesus.

This is the sense of C. S. Lewis's novel *Till We Have Faces*.[28] Psyche puzzles over the silence of God and agonizes that God does not clean up the world's chaos and make truth plain. She despairs of an answer at first and suspects God—if a God there be—of cruelty. But in the end she realizes that God intends to draw the meaning of self precisely from self, a painful birth process, to guarantee that one's life with God is still truly one's own.

We are not capable of removing the veil on our own; it is the operation of the Spirit, a "grace," in the words of Gregory of Nyssa, "that the eye might be free of any impediment and thus gaze unhindered at that beloved Beauty."[29] The life task, therefore, is this: by the power of the Spirit to find and develop the true face, the unveiled face, with which to meet the face of God, which will yet be more fully revealed. It is an ongoing process whereby we clothe ourselves "with the new self, which is being renewed in knowledge according to the image of its creator" (Colossians 3:10).

CHANGING FROM GLORY TO GLORY

In 2 Corinthians 3:18, Paul offers a deepening and clarifying vision of divinity. Increased understanding also takes the form of personal transformation: the faithful, by steady contemplation of the "splendor of the Lord," come to share in that splendor. Simone Weil understands this: "One of the principal truths of Christianity, a truth that goes almost unrecognized today, is that looking is what saves us."[30] We become what we behold. Joseph Sittler speaks of the ability not simply to see but to behold. To behold something is to see in and through it the mystery of God.[31]

The Orthodox Christian world has long known the power of holy images. In the icon the devout worshiper sees not a mere devotional picture or a visual representation of some significant event or person, but a divine archetype. The New Testament speaks of Christ as the true icon of God, the one through whom the iconic presence of God is revealed. Once in the form of God by the power of the Spirit, the eternal Christ came to share our form and make possible our glorious transformation that one day we might see fully.

"Glory" never can be achieved by human effort alone; the old gospel hymn "O, That Will Be Glory for Me" trivializes Paul's significant meditation on the glory of God revealed in Jesus Christ by the Spirit, who together reveal and mediate glory. The knowledge of glory is discovered in the face of Jesus

(2 Corinthians 4:6), into whose likeness we are being changed. Incorporation into Christ by the power of the Spirit transfers glory to the believer; in other words, God invites our participation in the divine life. Paul characterizes the pneumatic life of transformation into the resurrection likeness/image of Christ as a metamorphosis of glory (2 Corinthians 3:18).[32]

It is easy for us to desire to share in the glory of the exalted Christ, seated with God in the heavenlies, but this is not the primary way that Christic glory is disclosed; rather, it is cruciform. Weil observes that the true glory of Christianity is found in Jesus' cry of absolute despair, "*Eli, Eli, lema sabachthani?*" (Matthew 27:46),[33] which solidified his identity with our own suffering and abandonment. Becoming like him, attaining resurrection from the dead, requires that we follow the pathway of voluntary displacement, where sacredness and vulnerability are close. We recall the perceptive insight of Mother Teresa as she spoke of encountering the Christ in the "poorest of the poor." While not yet seeing face to face, this beholding both deepens and clarifies the mystery of *Deus absconditus*,[34] "the hidden God" who is the Spirit.

SEEING FACE TO FACE

As persons who image the triune life of God, we understand ourselves in terms of certain constitutive relationships: with God, with other people, and with the earth and its living creatures. Spiritual formation, therefore, is not individualistic, but a relational, communal concept that beckons us really to see one another. Spiritual formation is not focused on the "self"—the preoccupation of rationalistic, individualistic modernity.[35]

Bearing the image of God depends upon both a mutual relationality with others and an abiding friendship with God. Being created in the image of the triune God means, in Marjorie Suchocki's words, being "called to an existence with 'perforated boundaries.'"[36] "Perforated boundaries" speaks of an openness regarding human personhood, a willingness to experience oneself as unfinished. We do not ground our own becoming; rather, that is the fructifying work of God's Spirit as well as other humans God has given to us to form our lives. Indeed, the image of perforated boundaries is permeable, suggesting "continuous transformation through the mutuality of relation," and that "openness to the other affects the primary identity formation of all."[37] It is God's openness to otherness that sustains Trinitarian relations. God's being as Trinitarian communion (a thoroughly spiritual reality) is the ontological ground of human personhood in community. As John Zizioulas argues, human beings in communion with God are transformed into a new mode of existence that allows persons to transcend the "boundaries of the self" in order to be free to become fully personal, as well as a genuine expression of ecstasies toward communion.[38] It is by the Spirit that humans participate in the *perichoresis* of the divine life.

Biblical theology speaks of "seeing face to face" as delighting in the fullness of presence, God's and our own. Such clarity of vision and communion occurs after a lifetime of learning to pay attention to the mode of God's presence, however elusive. It will not occur otherwise, because, as Simone Weil claims, "Attention is the only faculty of the soul that gives us access to God."[39]

Thus, we must learn to pay attention to the formative work of the Spirit in our lives, so that we might share the movement to "finish, then, thy new creation,"[40] in the words of Wesley's beloved hymn. Wendy Wright reminds us that the life of contemplation (a life of sustained attention) is "that radical and risky opening of self to be changed by and, in some way, into God's own self. It is a formative life; it changes us and our perceptions."[41] It is a life of continual dying, of being stripped over and over again of the comfortable and familiar, of letting go and allowing a reality beyond our own to shape us. This may be a painful process, but the Spirit works gently in our lives to make us both fully God's and fully ourselves.

Gregory of Nyssa's vision of the Christian life, in keeping with his fourth-century ethos, was one of moving from "glory to glory." He fervently believed that humankind was created to be made one with God. Human life is a progressive movement toward God-likeness, a concentration on and unification with the divine. This is effected in stages of spiritual growth, a sort of perpetual re-creation, a constant beginning again at ever more transformed levels of being. One never "arrives" in this process, but plunges deeper and deeper into divine darkness, the mystery of God; each "glory," or stage of the journey, when reached, gives way to the next "glory," which rises up beyond.[42] The Spirit is the efficient cause of this transformation, ever laboring to help Christians reflect the likeness of Jesus.

Nathaniel Hawthorne's short story "The Great Stone Face" offers a wonderful portrayal of transformation into another's likeness through beholding. Hawthorne tells of Ernest, who lived in a small village across the valley from a magnificent, almost divine, visage that jutted out from the rock face of the mountains. As a child, Ernest heard the prophecy that someday a great man who bore a close resemblance to the expansive, generous face would come to the village. Ernest took the story seriously and spent much time contemplating what sort of man this might be, as he gazed reflectively across the valley.

The years passed, and three men of renown came to the village, each acclaimed by the people as the one who fulfilled the prophecy. Each time, Ernest was profoundly disappointed, both by the gullibility of the townspeople and by the visitors' lack of resemblance to the kind and loving figure with whom he conversed daily. It was his passion, deliberately emulating the beneficent character he observed in the great stone face.

Ernest continued to mature and became a preacher whose wisdom and profound perceptions about people were known far beyond his close-knit community. One day a poet came to the village, intent on meeting Ernest, whose reputation had reached him far away. By fortuitous circumstance, Ernest had read much of the writer's poetry and was immensely grateful for the artistry that shone through his works. After pleasant, mutually appreciative conversation, the poet accompanied Ernest to his usual post for preaching, an outdoor gathering place where the villagers eagerly awaited his thoughtful remarks, As the faithful villager stood in his pulpit, with the great stone face on the mountain behind him, the poet suddenly exclaimed, "Behold! Behold! Ernest is himself the likeness of the Great Stone Face!"[43] All the people, who earlier had deluded themselves into thinking that others fulfilled the prophecy, now realized that Ernest was the one who truly bore the image. Ernest was less convinced and walked homeward slowly, "still hoping that some wiser and better man than himself would by and by appear."[44]

When is our presence "finished"? Traditional eschatology has followed the first Johannine epistle: "When he is revealed, we will be like him, for we will see him as he is" (1 John 3:2). Thus, our lives, hidden with Christ in God, finally reflect the glory that is ours by the work of the Spirit, who fits us to participate in the divine community of overflowing grace, in which we are fully at home. Thus the presence of God and the presence of all made welcome by God find fulfillment in the everlasting communion suffused with the glory of God.

And so we at last may sing with all Christians these words from a ninth-century Latin hymn:

Bring us with your saints to behold your great beauty,
There to see you, Christ our God, throned in great glory;

There to possess heaven's peace and joy, your truth and
love.
For endless ages of ages, world without end.[45]

NOTES

1. Selected passages in this chapter are reprinted from Molly T. Marshall,
"Spiritual Formation: Humanity as Unfinished Presence," in *Freedom of
Conscience*, ed. Paul D. Simmons (Amherst, N.Y.: Prometheus Press, 2000),
194–203.

2. The term synergism often suggests that persons are saved by their own
work rather than by grace. That is not the meaning I have in mind. I am using
the term as a way of accentuating the responsibility that believers have "to live
their lives in the power of the Spirit," as James Dunn puts it (*The Christ and
the Spirit: Collected Essays of James D. G. Dunn*, vol. 2 [Grand Rapids:
Eerdmans, 1998], 14).

3. This information is drawn from "Giving the World a Peek," *U.S. News
and World Report*, June 9, 1997, 14.

4. See Dorothy C. Bass, ed., *Practicing Our Faith: A Way of Life for a
Searching People* (San Francisco: Jossey-Bass, 1997).

5. Wuthnow describes the shifts in perspectives and practices of spirituality
among Americans in recent decades in *After Heaven: Spirituality in America
since the 1950s* [Berkeley and Los Angeles: University of California Press, 1998).

6. For a comparative view of differing ecclesial views of sanctification, see
Donald L. Alexander, ed., *Christian Spirituality: Five Views of Sanctification*
(Downers Grove, Ill.: InterVarsity, 1998).

7. See Molly T. Marshall, "The Changing Face of Baptist Discipleship,"
Review and Expositor 95, no. 1 (winter 1998): 64.

8. Mark S. Burrows, "'There the Dance Is': The Dynamics of Spirituality in
a Turning World," *American Baptist Quarterly 16*, no. 1 (March 1997): 6.

9. See *Nature and Grace: Selections from the Summa Theologica of Thomas
Aquinas*, trans. and ed. A. M. Fairweather (Philadelphia: Westminster, 1954),
35–49.

10. Colin E. Gunton, *The One, the Three and the Many: God, Creation and
the Culture of Modernity* (Cambridge: Cambridge University Press, 1993), 182.

11. Margaret R. Miles, *Practicing Christianity: Critical Perspectives for an
Embodied Spirituality* (New York: Crossroad, 1990), 75.

12. Scholars of the "Christ Hymn" of Philippians 2 have long commented
on the contrast between our human parents' grasping of what was forbidden
and Jesus Christ's relinquishment of what was naturally the possession of the
eternal Son. See especially Ralph P. Martin, *Carmen Christi: Philippians II.5-11*

in Recent Interpretation and in the Setting of Early Christian Worship, rev. ed. (Grand Rapids: Eerdmans, 1983).

13. See Miroslav Volf, *Exclusion and Embrace: A Theological Exploration of Identity, Otherness, and Reconciliation* (Nashville: Abingdon, 1996), which challenges humanity's propensity to resist and exclude "otherness" as contrary to the gospel.

14. George T. Montague first made this connection for me (*Holy Spirit: Growth of a Biblical Tradition* [Peabody, Mass.: Hendrickson, 1976], 57–58).

15. *The Enchiridion on Faith, Hope and Love*, trans. J. F. Shaw, ed. Henry Paolucci (Chicago: Regnery Gateway, 1961), 135.

16. Blaise Pascal, *Pensées*, trans. A. J. Krailsheimer (New York: Penguin Books, 1966), 585.

17. Samuel Terrien sketches the contradictions of the biblical presentation of the presence and absence of God in *The Elusive Presence: Toward a New Biblical Theology* (San Francisco: Harper & Row, 1978).

18. Walter Brueggemann, *Old Testament Theology: Essays on Structure, Theme, and Text*, ed. Patrick D. Miller Jr. (Minneapolis: Fortress, 1992), 152–161. Brueggemann also notes the neglect in contemporary spirituality of the correlative relationship between Yahweh's presence and obedience in the Mosaic tradition.

19. Stephanie Paulsell, "Honoring the Body," in Bass, ed., *Practicing Our Faith*, 15.

20. Peter C. Hodgson, *God in History: Shapes of Freedom* (Nashville: Abingdon, 1989), 36.

21. Mark C. Taylor, *Erring: A Postmodern A/theology* (Chicago: University of Chicago Press, 1984), cited in Hodgson, *God in History*, 36.

22. Gregory of Nyssa reflected at length on Moses' request and the divine response: letting Moses see God's back. He writes, "By this I think we are taught that he who wishes to see God, will see his Beloved only by constantly following after Him, and the contemplation of His face is really the unending journey towards Him" (*From Glory to Glory: Texts from Gregory of Nyssa's Mystical Writings*, trans. and ed. Herbert Musurillo [New York: Charles Scribner's Sons, 1961], 263).

23. See the *Heidelberg Theses* (1518), W, I, 361–363.

24. Annie Dillard, *Pilgrim at Tinker Creek* (New York: Harper's Magazine Press, with Harper & Row, 1974), 205.

25. Brueggemann, *Old Testament Theology*, 152.

26. I am indebted to Brueggemann's treatment for the basic outline of this argument.

27. My own theological formation is indelibly stamped by the constructive insights of Prof. John A. T. Robinson of Trinity College, Cambridge University. This expression comes from his Christology, *The Human Face of God*

(Philadelphia: Westminster, 1973).

28. C. S. Lewis, *Till We Have Faces: A Myth Retold* (New York: Harcourt, Brace, 1956).

29. Gregory of Nyssa, *From Glory to Glory*, 264.

30. Simone Weil, *Waiting for God*, trans. Emma Craufurd (New York: Capricorn Books, 1959), 36.

31. Joseph Sittler, *Gravity and Grace: Reflections and Provocations*, ed. Linda-Marie Delloff (Minneapolis: Augsburg, 1986), 16. Wendy Wright observes, "To gaze is to open our mind and, even more deeply, our heart, to the evocative symbolism, the continually self-revealing forms of the icon and the deep truths encoded there" ("Living into the Image: Thoughts on Religious Imagination and the Imagery of Tradition," *Weavings* 12, no. 1 [January/February 1997], 15).

32. Helpful to this analysis has been Carey C. Newman, *Paul's Glory-Christology: Tradition and Rhetoric* (Leiden: Brill, 1992).

33. Weil, *Waiting for God*, 5.

34. This term is based on Isaiah 45:15, often used by Martin Luther to indicate that a knowledge of God can come only through God's self-revelation, since God is "hidden" from our reason by human finitude and sin.

35. See Stanley Hauerwas, "The Sanctified Body: Why Perfection Does Not Require a 'Self,'" in *Embodied Holiness: Toward a Corporate Theology of Spiritual Growth*, ed. Samuel M. Powell and Michael E. Lodahl (Downer's Grove, Ill.: InterVarsity, 1999), 19–38.

36. Majorie Suchocki, "Theological Foundations for Ethnic and Gender Diversity in Faculties or Excellence and the Motley Crew," *Theological Education* 26, no. 2 (1990): 43.

37. Ibid.

38. John Zizioulas, *Being as Communion* (Crestwood, N.Y.: St. Vladimir's Seminary Press, 1985), 41, 43, 53–65.

39. Cited by Diogenes Allen, *Spiritual Theology: The Theology of Yesterday for Spiritual Help Today* (Cambridge: Cowley, 1997), 82.

40. These words begin the last verse of Charles Wesley's hymn "Love Divine, All Loves Excelling."

41. Wendy M. Wright, "Contemplation in Time of War," *Weavings* 7, no. 4 (July/August 1992): 22.

42. Gregory of Nyssa, *From Glory to Glory*, 29.

43. *Greatest Short Stories*, vol. 1 (New York: P. F. Collier, 1953), 120.

44. Ibid.

45. *Ubi Caritas*, trans. Richard Proulx, GIA Publications, Inc. (used by permission).

CHAPTER 7

WINNOWING THE HARVEST

To each is given the manifestation of the Spirit
for the common good.
—1 Corinthians 12:7

Do not quench the Spirit. Do not despise the words
of prophets, but test everything.
—1 Thessalonians 5:19-21

Beloved, do not believe every spirit, but test the spirits
to see whether they are from God.
—1 John 4:1

WE HAVE STUDIED THE WORK OF THE SPIRIT IN UNIVERSAL AND
particular ways. The Spirit not only vivifies all of creation, but
also indwells and empowers certain communities and individuals for more discrete tasks. The Spirit is ever bringing newness in
creaturely life and human structures, which provides avenues to
participate in God's great mission with the world. In this chapter
we explore ways that the Spirit continues the perichoretic dance,
drawing us into the movement of the triune life of God. By delineating varied manifestations of spiritual power, we will discover
further the Spirit's rhythm.

Scripture exhorts believers to exercise discernment in charac-
terizing the work of the Spirit. Liberally scattered throughout the
hortatory sections of the Bible are cautionary notes about "testing the spirits" in order to avoid facile conclusions about the
activity of the Spirit. All that purports to be "spiritual" may not

be in keeping with the ways of God as Spirit, but determining this can prove elusive. Sometimes subtle and other times unmistakable, the Spirit lists her way in the world.

This chapter uses the metaphor of winnowing to help us discriminate between authentic and fraudulent claims for the activity of the Spirit. To that end, we will study the Spirit's gifting for service, our task of discerning the spirits, and the work we share with the Spirit in liberating from oppression and laboring toward the reign of God. The goal of the Spirit is to winnow in order to produce a great harvest of justice and peace through the lives of those empowered by the dynamic presence of God.

GIFTING FOR SERVICE

As we have seen in the last three chapters, the Spirit overshadows our lives and joins us to the Christ and to one another. The Spirit makes God present to us and forms us into the likeness of the self-giving God. Prior to speaking about "gifts of the Spirit," we should speak of the "gift of the Spirit." It is a generous grace that the Spirit chooses to abide in our lives and in our midst. The very presence of Spirit is gift. How can we describe the effects of this dynamic presence? Unstintingly given,[1] the Spirit of God sifts the wheat of our lives for sowing in God's field. The Spirit is God's empowerment for service, which the New Testament describes as "spiritual gifts" or *charismata*, "gifts of grace."

Are there gifts that come to us in our baptism that we did not possess prior to that new birth, or does the Spirit bring to flower what is already there? Actually, both occur. When "we were all baptized into one body," we were made to "drink of one Spirit" (1 Corinthians 12:13). This suggests that further endowment with the Spirit accompanies our baptism; we experience a new fullness of divine presence, although the Spirit has continually held us in trust for God as persons sustained by the divine breath.

Unmistakably, however, a new experience in the Spirit occurs as we are sown with Christ (John 12:24) and become a part of his fruitful life as an integral member of his body. What is already a part of our lives undergoes a process of winnowing so that what is of little consequence can be blown away as chaff and good grain might remain.

We may rightly ask: how does the one *charis* (the Spirit) become the diverse *charismata* (gifts of the Spirit) by which the body functions? The interests and capacities we have by genetic disposition and environmental opportunity are given new energy and direction by the breath of the Spirit, who sustains us through the waters of baptism. Raised to walk in newness of life, we express our baptismal identity in Christ through varieties of service. Everyone is gifted by the same Spirit, hence all Christians are "charismatic," but the manifestations are widely disparate, albeit working in concert. Giftedness is distinctive within the organic expression of the people of God, yet all is held in common, for the Spirit is given to all equally.

Are the gifts we use in the service of the church different from the gifts we use in our other work? In other words, what makes a gift spiritual? Jürgen Moltmann helps correct some misconceptions about the nature of spiritual gifts by linking call and endowment, *klēsis* and *charisma*.[2] Instead of opposing natural gifts to spiritual gifts, he sees that when a person is called (1 Corinthians 7:17),[3] God "puts their whole life at the service of his [sic] coming kingdom, which renews the world."[4] When offered to Christ, all gifts become charges, and nothing can be called unclean.[5] Powers and energies that a person might regard as mundane can become instruments of the Spirit. Within the body of Christ, one's gifts can be sparked by their interaction with others, as together they strengthen the community for service.

A seminary student[6] at the school where I teach illustrates this movement of reclaiming gifts that once were serving the nefarious machinations of the world. A gifted salesman, he learned that much profit was to be made selling drugs on the streets of Kansas City. A handsome and winsome figure, he drew many other young men around him to further his illegal activities. And he prospered, until arrested and sent to prison, twice. There he met the One who had not ceased loving and calling him. He made a commitment to start over and allow himself to be God's instrument.

Upon his release from prison, he took stock of what he needed to do. He needed to go back to school, which he did. He needed to settle old debts, which he managed to do. And he needed to find another line of work. He became an industrious and successful insurance broker. In giving witness to his story of redemption, he laughingly says, "I'm still selling stuff, only now it's legal!" The gifts were the same, but now they were put to constructive purposes, in the power of the renewing Spirit, who gave him his life back. Actually, the Spirit made new all of his life.

One of the issues challenging him as he pursues theological education is where to offer his ministry. He moves freely in the world of prostitutes and crack houses; he goes there because he knows the great need that dwells there. He is not reticent about sharing his faith in contexts that might intimidate others. Preaching in prison and counseling convicts, he bears strong testimony to God's desire to take all that we are and allow the Spirit to quicken it for service. From experience he testifies that no aspect of a person's life is off limits to the refining fire of God's Spirit. Yet he wonders, is it really vocational ministry if it is offered outside the walls of the church? I assure him that it is and that his own story uniquely prepares him for such ministry. Indeed, it may be where the Spirit is moving most freely.[7]

Our theology of spiritual gifts has suffered from the same preoccupation with individualism that plagues our theology of salvation.[8] We have placed primary stress on the unique expression of the Spirit in each person's life and have neglected the New

Testament's emphasis on the interdependence of the gifts. The Pauline image of the church as the body of Christ, with varied yet unified activities, should inform what we say about the gifts of the Spirit.

Possession is the wrong word to use about spiritual giftedness. We do not possess the gifts; rather, they gather our lives into new dimensions of meaning through service. Years ago, I gained an important theological insight about individuals and their gifts from a rather unlikely source: an episode of the 1970s sitcom *The Love Boat*. Two ballet dancers, Klaus and Joanna, are on the cruise. One afternoon, while discussing their future plans as dance partners, Klaus abruptly announces, "I am too old for the rigors of the dance tour. I am not going to continue to dance." Joanna, unnerved by the threat of losing her partner, retorts, "If you are not going to dance, then I will not dance either!" Captain Stubing, standing on the deck above (did he ever steer the ship?), overhears the conversation and invites the young ballerina to the bridge. He says, "Joanna, I have something to say to you. You cannot refuse to dance, because your gift belongs to everyone." Theological insight from a sitcom! We do not own or control the ultimate scattering of our gifts; they belong to everyone. So it is in the body of Christ: "To each is given the manifestation of the Spirit for the common good" (1 Corinthians 12:7). All the members must join the dance with the Spirit, sowing and reaping, to express God's beautiful movement in the world.

There are several listings of spiritual gifts in the New Testament, as well as accompanying instructions about their employment (e.g., 1 Corinthians 12:8-11,28-30; 14:1-5; Ephesians 4:11-12; 1 Peter 4:10-11). With our penchant for order, we try to rank them or decide which ones are still in effect long after the age of the apostles. Some of the gifts make us nervous, for they seem to call into question our reliance on rational explanations for certain phenomena.[9] For example, are there gifts for healing apart from medical science? Perhaps that is the wrong way to pose the question, for it pits natural and supernatural against one another in ways that seem to relegate spiritual power only to the mysterious or the irrational. Do we have to choose one or the other? I think not. There are signs of the reign of God—inexplicable healings—that cannot be discounted in a "world in which events beyond the scope or ken of our everyday experience occur."[10] Yet it is always a divine-human synergy. Marvelous advances in science, through which God gladly works, are signs of new creation. The Spirit is free to employ natural and supranatural means, working with and beyond human capacities. The world is still in a dynamic process of becoming, and many agents contribute to new events: past causes, divine purposes, and the activity of the involved subjects. This collaborative movement makes it difficult ever to speak of a single cause in bringing about a new event, for there is order and openness, indeterminacy as well as recognizable patterns.[11] The humility of God as Spirit is seen in the willingness to share causality; the glory of God as Spirit is that the fragility of creation can bear the weight of divine presence. Nothing in the world occurs apart from the power of God, but God is not the exclusive arbiter of power in the world. Our labor, our prayers, and our imaginative new insights are participants with God in doing "mighty works."

Baptists have a rather ambivalent perspective on certain manifestations of the Spirit's power. There has been a concerted effort to domesticate the Spirit, making sure that giftedness is regulated through less-than-dramatic expressions. When fellow Baptists experience spiritual renewal that might issue in unusual (at least to their critics) practices in worship—such as raising hands, dancing for joy, anointing with oil for healing, or speaking in a language of prayer that others cannot understand—they are often accused of excess. James McClendon reminds us that the religious witness of many of our Baptist forebears "was greeted with general derision when it first appeared."[12] Currently, many scholars contend for the authenticity of ecstasy and fellowship expressed by the pentecostal wing of Christianity; moreover, they believe that the Spirit is seeking to kindle such renewal in the varied communions, Orthodox, Catholic, and Protestant alike.[13] We should welcome experiences that allow our spirits to soar.

Caution is in order, however, when advocating freedom in the manifestation of *charismata*. We should not expect to soar all the time. Some interpreters have attempted to traverse the centuries between early Christianity and the present without proper attention to the contextualization of these grace gifts. It seems that some gifts may have a greater appropriateness in certain historical contexts.[14] Certainly the miracle of speaking and hearing other languages on the day of Pentecost was necessary for the effective proclamation of the gospel. More needed in our day is a ready hearing of new voices through a greater awareness of the Spirit's gifting of those long excluded from ecclesial leadership.[15] Furthermore, we must remember that the primary witnesses to the Spirit's gifting, Luke and Paul, were writing in different epochs, addressing different ecclesial needs. Paul wrote to temper the enthusiasm of young mission churches whose excessive claims for the Spirit threatened a coherent witness. Luke, writing in a later period, was urging churches that had lost their missionary zeal to seek the Spirit.[16] Paul's approach stresses the gift of the Spirit given in baptism; Luke's approach suggests that one must earnestly seek the Spirit as an additional endowment after conversion.[17] Pentecostals have tended to follow the trajectory of Luke-Acts and thus have separated baptism with water from baptism with the Spirit.[18] This two-stage pattern of salvation distinguishes between the converted (the "saved" or "born again") and the sanctified (having received a "second blessing" or "baptism in the Spirit").[19] Historically, the wider church has followed the view advocated in the Pauline writings: We receive the Spirit when we are baptized into Christ. Furthermore, Paul does not limit sanctification to only a few, but sees it as the gradual transformation of all Christians (1 Corinthians 1:2).

Luke regularly links the coming of the Spirit with tongues and prophesying as a way to reassure the church that the Spirit will empower it to fulfill its missionary task. This view has led Pentecostals (falsely, in my judgment) to view tongues as the *sine qua non* of the Spirit's presence. Paul, in marked contrast, recognizes the working of the Spirit in ways that are not deemed extraordinary in nature—for example, service, exhortation, acts of mercy, even being married or single. Walter Hollenweger observes that Paul "strongly refutes the widespread religious conception that the unusual, the supernatural, is more divine."[20]

Is there a way to hold these distinctive perspectives in tension? The discord between the Pauline and Lukan approaches contributes to the "symphonic pluralism"[21] of the Bible. When one apostolic voice is privileged and another silenced, the church abdicates its ever-present task of discerning spiritual guidance for today's faithful witness. There is wisdom to be gained about the Spirit's gifting from each of these literary witnesses, and they must be read together, for they offer insight about order and enthusiasm, yearning for the Spirit and relying on the presence already given.

It is well known that the charismatic movement is flourishing widely today, not only in the traditions more identified as pentecostal.[22] Perhaps this is because persons are longing for new forms of experiential worship and believe they can find room for the Spirit in the free-flowing movement of less liturgical contexts. Yet I would resist the notion that certain forms of worship are somehow "more spiritual," more suffused with Spirit. What makes the difference, in my judgment, is the clear acknowledgment that divine presence has called the assembly together and the corporate anticipation of the movement of the Spirit in all the acts of worship: gathering, praying, communing and baptizing, reading Scripture, proclaiming, singing, welcoming, and blessing. As the praxis-oriented Paul instructs, all are to come ready to offer themselves through "a hymn, a lesson, a revelation, a tongue, or an interpretation…all for building up" (1 Corinthians 14:26).

While some Christians are absorbed with trying to discern the relative importance of their gifts, others are persuaded that somehow they were passed over by the Spirit. Both approaches counter the testimony of Scripture. All are gifted, and every manifestation of grace is necessary. The apostle Paul is adamant about seeking the higher expressions of the Spirit's presence, a "more excellent way" (1 Corinthians 12:31), rather than wrangling over positions of prominence according to the "workings" of the Spirit. A fundamental humility is necessary in this: gifts are given; no one has them all; each depends upon the others, whether "weaker" or "less respectable." Indeed, all *charisms* "serve inclusion and participation in the knowledge of God mediated by the Spirit."[23]

Another way the New Testament speaks of gifting for service is through the image of fruit. A cumulative logic informs the apostolic writings as they move from discussing gifts, which are distinctive expressions of Spirit, to fruit (Galatians 5:22-23; Colossians 1:10; cf. John 15:1-16), which involves common manifestations of Spirit in maturing Christians. Indeed, the fruit of the Spirit is the means by which giftedness can be employed without rancor. One may have the gift of prophetic speech, but unless one "speaks the truth in love," that gift most likely will not serve the common good, "each part working properly" (Ephesians 4:15-16).

The Spirit's presence in believers' lives causes them to flower and bear fruit in productive ways. This fruit may be described as graceful demonstrations of the Spirit's presence—for example, peace, kindness, joy, generosity, or the enduring fruit of new disciples, friends of Jesus.[24] The abiding of Christ through the Spirit makes Christians fruitful and allows them to function interdependently.

DISCERNING THE SPIRITS

How do we know when certain practices violate the patterns of the Spirit's movement in the world? Are there measures or tests that can lead us to clear discernment? Already we have discovered some of the criteria for proper use of gifts: we are not to despise the gifts, in whatever form they might come; we are not to quench the Spirit; we are to use *charismata* for the common good; we are to exercise our gifts in fruitful ways, always tempered by the Spirit. These admonitions are clear and help us in discernment. There is, however, a further challenge: "Test the spirits to see whether they are from God" (1 John 4:1).

The Johannine language is quite different from that of Paul. Whereas Paul enjoins the Corinthian Christians to discern the (good) spirits among them, all of which are manifestations of the Holy Spirit, the writer of the first Johannine epistle reminds the church that "spirit" does not simply refer to the Spirit of God.[25] A spirit also pervades the world that seeks to negate the importance of Christ: the spirit of the Antichrist.[26] There is the spirit of truth, and there is the spirit of deceit; hence, Christians must "test" the spirits.

These epistles were written during a time of schism, with one group of formerly Johaninne Christians being anathematized for becoming secessionists. Their departure is seen by those who remain in the fold as apostasy, following another "Spirit." It is hard to reconstruct all that was going on in the ruptured community, but probably it related to a debate concerning how "what Jesus was or did in the flesh was related to his being the Christ."[27] Thus the Christological confession of the secessionists was docetic in nature, and according to Johannine Christianity did not reflect the Spirit that belongs to God. "By this you know the Spirit of God: every spirit that confesses that Jesus Christ has come in the flesh is from God, and every spirit that does not confess Jesus is not from God. And this is the spirit of the antichrist, of which you have heard that it is coming; and now it is already in the world" (1 John 4:2-3). Authentic Christological confession is made possible by the Spirit, as a theological reading of this passage illustrates. Baptism entailed confessing Jesus Christ and receiving the Holy Spirit, and consistent confession is dependent upon the S/spirit that comes from God—God's Spirit and the Christian's spirit.[28] Johannine theology, in both Gospel and Epistle, sees bearing witness to Christ as a Spirit-empowered activity (John 15:26-27; 1 John 5:6).

The problem faced by the Johannine community recurs throughout history. In struggling to discern who is being faithful to the tradition "once received," churches often splinter. Christopher Morse wisely perceives that faith in the Holy Spirit is a "refusal to deify human subjectivity."[29] By ourselves, we do not know what a "lying spirit" is and where truth lies. Only the Spirit of God can guide us into all truth. Is it possible for the Spirit to help us bear the strain of our differences, or should we part ways when oppositional views grow unyielding?

As a fledgling youth minister, fresh out of college with a major in psychology, I ran headlong into a situation in which the need for spiritual discernment greatly outstripped my experience. A committed couple in the church, who were leaders in the youth group and the parents of two small children, began to yearn for a deeper experience of the Spirit. Believing that the Baptist church (where the pastor and I were the only full-time staff members) was not "spiritual enough," they began to attend some charismatic meetings in an adjoining community. Soon, new phrases began to crop up in their language of faith. They spoke of "taking authority over demons," of their "prayer language," and of doing "greater works" than those in the days of Jesus, as they believed he promised. The pastor was perplexed over the situation, not wanting to curtail what seemed to be genuine spiritual hunger. The couple began holding special meetings in their home in which the topic often turned to criticism of the pastor (and the youth minister) for lacking "the baptism of the Spirit." The youth were, understandably, confused. I was unsure how to be a reliable guide in this. The pastor began exercising pastoral authority with them, forbidding them from instructing the youth with their newfound insights, believing that by disciplining this couple, the unity of the larger body was preserved. Not surprisingly, they left the church.

I left as well, not long after. I knew it was time for me to pursue theological education if I was to minister effectively. This experience taught me that I was not at all prepared for issues of this magnitude. I had no way to discern who was being led by the Spirit: the pastor or the couple. I plunged into my seminary studies with an urgent learning readiness.

A few weeks into that first semester, word came to me about a grievous situation. The couple, in their genuine goodness, had invited a teenaged girl from a nearby treatment center to live with them as a part of their family. One day, they left her alone with one of the children, a little girl, whom she brutally killed. In shock, they began to tell their extended family, as well as the faith communities of which they were a part, that God would perform a miracle and raise their daughter from the dead. "Doesn't Scripture teach us that we have authority over death, illness, and all sorts of evil? Doesn't Scripture teach us that if two agree on anything in heaven or on earth, it will be done for them? Didn't Jesus say that we would have power to call the dead to life?"

They went to the funeral believing that before the service was over, little "Ashley" would climb out of her casket. Those in attendance did not know how to pray, what to believe, or how to comfort distraught parents whose faith led them to the precipice of presumption. Their exhortations to their daughter to arise finally fell silent, and they proceeded with the service of committal.

Discerning the movement of the Spirit in this story is a complex challenge, for the currents are mixed. The family's desire to deepen their spiritual experience was commendable, but the ensuing spiritual pride and antagonism toward their pastor were ill advised. The pastor was wise to try to offer guidance to the larger congregation, but did he take too hard a line with these whose faith was searching yet less formed? Was he threatened that this couple was experiencing the Spirit in an extraecclesial context, where he had little influence? The fruit of generous hospitality toward a troubled adolescent was evidence of the Spirit's work in their hearts, but they ignored warnings from others about the possible dangers—they simply believed in God's protection. Still young Christians themselves, they assumed that they could replicate any of the miracles recorded in Scripture upon demand. If they said the right words or prayed with enough faith, God would be compelled to do what they requested. When the miracle they sought did not occur, their faith was crushed.

Spiritual discernment is fraught with uncertainty, even danger, for it can be either "prophetically subversive or grossly self-deceptive."[30] This stark reality should beckon patience and humility for all concerned. Quick to place blame or to think in polarizing ways, we condemn without understanding and draw conclusions based upon insights too insular to perceive the Spirit's new horizon. No one group ever possesses all the truth or behaves in every circumstance according to the Spirit. Conflict can be an instrument of the Spirit, for it can hold promise for finding a common ground that moves persons to a new receptivity to otherness. Preserving harmony and peace is not the only action of Spirit; fanning the flames of dissent can refine simplistic understandings, tempering them toward maturity.

Morse calls Christians to practice "faithful disbelief." He means that when we believe in God, at the same time we must "disbelieve what is not of God."[31] This calls for the kind of critical reflection rarely seen in Christian groups. With our genuine desire to encourage every flicker of faith, we have difficulty admitting that not every spirit is of God. Worse, we often do not know how to distinguish what serves the cause of Christ. Morse's injunction is apt for our era that includes competing claims about what is truly spiritual and that lacks seasoned biblical interpretation.

Danny Morris and Charles Olsen, among others, are currently providing resources to assist churches in their urgent need to practice spiritual discernment.[32] They emphasize the need for communal discernment, because the Spirit "lives in and through the community, bringing power and enlightenment to the people of God."[33] The process they outline takes seriously biblical guidance and the church's rich heritage of discernment.[34] Although there is no formula that can guarantee we will get it right, the Spirit's guidance can emerge through intentional processes that seek to be attentive to the various dimensions of discernment.[35] Luke Timothy Johnson calls discernment a theological process that "enables humans to perceive their characteristically ambiguous experience as revelatory and to articulate such experiences in a narrative of faith."[36] In other words, the act of judging or testing is a collaborative work of the Spirit and human intelligence. Some are more gifted than others in this,[37] but it is the work of the entire community. The winnowing Spirit empowers people to "discern [or 'test'] what is the will of God—what is good and acceptable and perfect" (Romans 12:2).

Early in the Christian missionary movement, a decision had to be made about accepting the Gentiles fully into the new community. As Acts 15 records,[38] much face-to-face deliberation, a clear consensus on what is essential to Christian confession, mutual respect, and a willingness to overcome rigid legalism about certain practices known to be burdensome all contributed to making room for new brothers and sisters in the faith. The Spirit urged them to extend the boundaries of the people of God and legitimate the Gentile mission, which they did. Luke says that conclusions reached by the Jerusalem council "seemed good to the Holy Spirit and to us" (Acts 15:28). Such is the result of discernment undertaken in the power and "ground of our meeting"[39] that the Spirit is.

LIBERATING FROM OPPRESSION

The winnowing work of the Spirit not only sifts the lives of Christians, but also labors toward the liberation of all oppressed. Those who are evil cannot endure the relentless wind of the Spirit, which drives the chaff away (Psalm 1:4).[40] Thought to carry weight in the world, oppressors really have "lightness of being" when confronted by the powerful gale of God's Spirit.

Lee Snook writes of "the rhetoric of reversal" when describing how the Spirit is overcoming evil in the world. This reversal takes the form of converting the human heart and mind "from twisted forms of love that consume the good, misrepresent the truth, and use beauty to mask abuses of power."[41] Our world is groaning under the burden of oppression, born of insatiable self-interest. Economically privileged Christians preoccupy themselves with trivia and ignore the "weightier matters" (Matthew 23:23). Tonghou Ngong David, a native of Cameroon, writes in poetry,

Amid the new, we are pushed to the corner,
We are Left Behind!
(What a mockery of a movie,
That looks above and abandons us next door!)
Our women and children die of fever,
AIDS ransacks our frail bodies,
While the world flies on....[42]

Pharmaceutical companies reap astronomical profits at the expense of our elders and the poor everywhere. Developing nations decimated by HIV-AIDS have little or no access to the drug therapies that are currently proving effective. The global proliferation of war strangles economies, leaving little for health and education needs. The oppressive hegemony of debt paralyzes countries such as Nicaragua, Haiti, and Guatemala. Desperately poor, they indenture their finest resources to the rapacious appetites of North American corporations. And, in the words of Gustavo Paràjon, the "avalanche of the North against the South" continues.[43]

Closer to home, we read daily of corrupt corporate executives who have put personal profit above ethics. They have deliberately lied about their company's finances and left others to clean up scandalous practices that filled their pockets while jeopardizing the financial future of their employees. Government policies, even in a democracy, too often increase rather than ease economic oppression of the vulnerable in our society.

Racial minorities continue to suffer oppression in a nation where the color of skin still matters more than the content of character decades after the prophetic leadership of Martin Luther King Jr. Suspicion shrouds young African American men, and often they feel defeated from the outset and live out the self-fulfilling prophecy of their discrimination.[44] Women remain vulnerable to life-threatening abuse; children often are treated as expendable commodities. Sexual minorities face ridicule and revulsion, rendering them fearful of making their truth known. This litany of oppression hardly exhausts the global groaning of the human family, not to mention the piercing cry of all creation.

Where is the "reversal" of which Snook writes occurring? How is it happening? How is the power of the Spirit at work? Answering these questions forces us to move beyond the traditional ascriptions of the Spirit's power. The Spirit is not just the inward work of God as advocate or intercessor, comforting and sustaining and transforming us within the body of Christ. The Spirit does not only indwell leaders of the people of God and the community of faith gathered around the cross. The cosmic work of the Spirit labors for the liberation of the world, even creation itself (a topic to be addressed in the final chapter).

The Spirit is at work in all forms of power in the world, but the Spirit cannot work unilaterally, because of the freedom granted to those whom God is beckoning to dance. The space in which God lets creation "be" is not overrun by divine determinism; it is a space for the dance partners, divine and human, to practice their steps that they might move in the rhythms of redemption.

The Spirit, as God's radical immanence, breathes through all structures—political, economic, educational, scientific, and so on. Nothing is too "secular" for the Spirit's winnowing work. Moreover, there is no special "religious" matrix where the Spirit can work in an unhindered way; the Spirit strains to find breathing room there as well. Listing through these varied instrumental means, the Spirit must tack through recalcitrant persons, pernicious systems, and even opposing powers.[45]

Two of the great liberative movements of the last two centuries in North America, Women's Rights and Civil Rights, are suffused with the Spirit's power. We recall feisty leaders such as Elizabeth Cady Stanton, Angelina Grimké, and Mary Lyon, whose faith in God and in themselves led them to proclaim equality long before

Congress enacted their desire for women's suffrage. By the middle of the nineteenth century, many women were calling for a different understanding of the biblical material. They began to realize that male interpreters used Scripture to reinforce their subjection; they needed to learn to read it for themselves and question "normative" interpretations.[46] Not only concerned for women's roles in church and society, they understood that other humans were being subjugated by the misappropriation of Scripture. Hence, many of the women who were advocates of women's rights also were active abolitionists.[47]

The Spirit's radical involvement in fallen human structures is evident in the Civil Rights Movement of the twentieth century. The prophet of the movement, Martin Luther King Jr., believed that the universe was on the side of justice. Although not explicitly naming the Spirit, his perception of what was at work in his fight for freedom carries the implication: "There is a creative force in this universe that works to bring the disconnected aspects of reality into a harmonious whole."[48] He understood that he experienced "cosmic companionship"[49] in this protracted struggle. While King rightly holds a place of preeminence, others presaged, accompanied, and furthered his mission.

It is hard to think of a person more filled with the power of the Spirit than Sojourner Truth—reformer, preacher, and exemplar of unwavering courage. Liberated from slavery in 1827, she spent the rest of her life involved in the "great reversal." Because of her witness, people had to think differently about what it means to "be a woman" and where the power of God is to be found. Only the power of the Spirit could enable her to preach that God was loving and kind, for she had suffered greatly at the hands of those who invoked God to keep her enslaved.[50] So empowered was she, that she expected that God would do what she requested; that is, her will and the Spirit's will had become one, as Paul observed happens in the lives of those in union with

the Spirit (1 Corinthians 6:17; cf. John 14:13-14). Contemporary womanist scholars reflect some of her spirit in their identification of the movement of the Spirit in the African American
community.[51] Literature, politics, arts, and medicine demonstrate the liberative work of empowered black women. Their
stories illumine the impulses of God's Spirit, freeing from the old
and creating the new.

These are but two examples of the Spirit's collaboration against
oppression, using the ingenuity and perseverance of "horizonal
persons"[52] who could see beyond the confines of their present
experience. Throughout the world, hopeful persons care for the
sick, distribute food, educate children, accompany the aging, and
work to change public policy, all in the power of the compassionate Spirit, who revives their energies and makes fruitful their
sowing for the future. The power of love subverts the power of
oppression, slowly but inexorably.

Sometimes the presence of the Spirit is evident in allowing persons to retain their humanity amidst life's squalor. The Spirit bub-
bles forth in laughter, even in the most degrading circumstances,
and eases the pain of the present trauma. Humor, that grace of
the Spirit, wells up when tears seem more in order. Even "gallows
humor" is a form of protest; while it makes light of tragic situa-
tions, it also issues a reminder that things are not the way they
ought to be.

Lee Snook, veteran theological teacher who spent many years
in Zimbabwe, writes about "destabilizing laughter" as a sign of
the Spirit. He contends that the power of the joke "aimed at
exposing...pretensions of power and authority"[53] is a form of
the power of Spirit—winnowing power, I believe. The Spirit
does not hesitate to poke fun at ecclesial structures whose self-
importance renders them inhospitable to lively currents.
Satirizing stiff forms of institutional authority is the Spirit's iron-
ic work;[54] this kind of humor usually is lost on those who prize

tradition even when it stultifies spiritual life. God's work in the church is deadly serious, they contend—sure enough, it does die when the ebullient laughter of the Spirit is silenced.

How does the power of the Spirit in the church work in tandem with the Spirit's movement in the world? In our day there is greater need for the church to perceive the ways in which the Spirit is at work beyond its regulated structures. Nicholas Healey suggests a new receptivity on the part of the church to the liberation occurring elsewhere:

> Since the church can at times learn from the work of the Spirit working in what is non-church, it seems reasonable to propose that the church should make a habit of listening to the non-church, of trying to discern the Spirit's action in its challenges, of seeking out its wisdom in case Christ's word is spoken there.[55]

To whom should the church be listening? Any structure or movement where persons are finding recovery, hope, and the stirrings of a new beginning is worthy of being heard. Whether it is in Alcoholics Anonymous, support groups for the HIV-infected, divorce recovery workshops, stimulating activities for handicapped persons, art therapy for children, or the privacy of the therapist's office, God's Spirit is seeking to move persons toward renewal of life. Spirit is the source of energy, the force field, for these action groups, these so-called self-help groups (actually, the Spirit is the helper *par excellence*, striving to make all things new). Christ's word is spoken when people are called from death to life; the Spirit's action is evident when healing of mind and spirit occur through compassionate companions.

The church has not always spoken words of grace to the broken, as such persons seem to represent failure or sin, and some Christians fear being tainted by association. Ideas of Christian perfection or a distorted theology of "reward and punishment" leave little room to welcome those who have not flourished (the "weak") in the same way as the successful (the "strong") within the flock.[56] Because suffering persons remind everyone of the frailty of the human condition, they often are sequestered and succumb to what Moltmann calls a "social death."[57] It is little wonder that persons seeking compassion and healing gravitate toward less judgmental contexts, where the Spirit may be more at liberty to lift oppression. The Spirit may also need to move toward more receptive channels, where winnowing occurs more freely. When the church observes these other fields as places where the Spirit is moving, may it repent and convert to a new humility and expansiveness.

Peter Hodgson suggests that this labor of the Spirit in liberating oppression is also for the "perfection (or freedom) of God."[58] He links the liberation of the world with the completion of the unfolding of the divine life. Through the Spirit, the triune figuration of God will renew the whole creation. The winnowing will be complete, and the God of the harvest will gather the wholesome grain into the garner evermore.[59] We will explore this consummating hope in the final chapter.

NOTES

1. John 3:34 speaks of God giving the Spirit "without measure."

2. Jürgen Moltmann, *The Spirit of Life: A Universal Affirmation*, trans. Margaret Kohl (Minneapolis: Fortress, 1992), 180.

3. The language of "calling" predominates in Pauline theology. It can mean calling to salvation (Romans 1:6), or the process of sanctification (1 Corinthians 1:2), or a particular vocation (1 Corinthians 7:20; Ephesians 4:1).

4. Moltmann, *The Spirit of Life*, 180.

5. Ibid., 182.

6. The student kindly granted me permission to use his story here.

7. See the interesting collection edited by Doris Donnelly, *Retrieving Charisms for the Twenty-First Century* (Collegeville, Minn.: Liturgical Press, 1999).

8. As I teach constructive theology, I always place soteriology after ecclesiology in order to stress that there is no such thing as solitary faith, as Wesley reminds us. We are invited to faith by the community of faith; we journey in faith with others for whom we are responsible and to whom we are accountable.

9. A key example is the phenomenon of *glossalalia*. How can we explain the continuing vitality of speaking in tongues long after the miracle of speaking and hearing at Pentecost? How does this "gift" function in one's personal life of prayer as well as in corporate worship? What kind of psychological processes are entailed in this kind of communication? Donald L. Gelpi, a Jesuit priest, seeks to answer these and other questions in a balanced treatment of the topic in *Pentecostalism: A Theological Viewpoint* (New York: Paulist Press, 1971), 144–145.

10. James W. McClendon Jr., *Systematic Theology*, Vol. 2 (Nashville: Abingdon, 1994), 438.

11. Ian G. Barbour's work has helped to shape my thinking in this area of causality. He writes, "I submit that it is in the biblical idea of the Spirit that we find the closest parallel to the process understanding of God's presence in the world" (*When Science Meets Religion: Enemies, Strangers, or Partners?* [San Francisco: HarperSanFrancisco, 2000], 176–177).

12. McClendon, *Systematic Theology*, 434.

13. Ibid., 437. See also the strong statements of Michael Welker, *God the Spirit*, trans. John F. Hoffmeyer (Minneapolis: Fortress, 1994), 238–239, and of Moltmann, *The Spirit of Life*, 186–188.

14. Wayne A. Grudem, ed., *Are Miraculous Gifts for Today?* (Grand Rapids: Zondervan, 1996), delineates four views on the current validity of the miraculous gifts specified in the New Testament, with a helpful survey of the topic in the evangelical world. In response to the question of whether healings, prophecies, and tongues are confined to the distant past or are authentic expressions of the Spirit's working in the churches today, the contributing authors offer four perspectives: The cessationist position argues that no such expressions of the gifts of the Spirit exist today; the other three positions—pentecostal, charismatic, and "third wave" (a renewal movement that arose in the 1980s)—with varying degrees of caution, encourage the use of all spiritual gifts today. In my view, these latter three designations are overly general, given the extent of Pentecostalism.

15. Letty M. Russell argues that restricting clergy status to men neither can be sustained by Scripture nor meet the needs of the contemporary church (*Church in the Round: Feminist Interpretation of the Church* [Louisville: Westminster John Knox, 1993], 49–54.) Although Baptists do not contend for a sacramental understanding of ordination in which a special endowment of Spirit is given by the laying on of hands, they affirm congregational discernment of the spiritual gifts needed for the work of ministry and believe that laying on

of hands both blesses and stirs up the gifts already given. American Baptists have been at the forefront of recognizing the calling and gifts of women for ministry; however, further advocacy is needed lest the church be found "fighting against God," as Gamaliel warned in Acts 5:39.

16. McClendon, *Systematic Theology: Doctrine*, vol. 2, 436, drawing from Walter J. Hollenweger, *The Pentecostals* (London: SCM, 1972), 336–341.

17. An example of this theology is Luke's probable emendation of Matthew's teaching about God giving "good things" to those who ask (7:11). In Luke's version (11:13), he substitutes "the Holy Spirit" for "good things." One must ask God for this gift, however; it is not presumed.

18. There is some warrant for this, in view of the proclamation of John the Baptist (Luke 3:16), and the narrative of Acts, where there is no consistent order of these four themes: hearing the gospel; accepting baptism in Jesus' name; receiving the Holy Spirit; and bearing faithful witness (cf. Acts 2:1-36; 2:37–7:60; 8:4-24; 9:1-30; 10:1-48; 19:1-6).

19. See Hollenweger, *The Pentecostals*, 322–323.

20. Hollenweger, *The Pentecostals*, 337.

21. I borrow this term from Robison B. James, "Beyond Old Habits and on to a New Land," in *Beyond the Impasse? Scripture, Interpretation, and Theology in Baptist Life*, ed. Robison B. James and David S. Dockery (Nashville: Broadman, 1992), 131.

22. This is especially true in Latin America. The charismatic movement is tied to the need for a liberative Spirit. See José Comblin, *The Holy Spirit and Liberation* (Maryknoll, N.Y.: Orbis, 1989) and Harvey Cox, *Fire from Heaven: The Rise of Pentecostal Spirituality and the Reshaping of Religion in the Twenty-first Century* (Reading, MA: Addison-Wesley, 1995).

23. Welker, *God the Spirit*, 241.

24. John 15:16: "And I appointed you to go and bear fruit, fruit that will last."

25. I draw this insight from Raymond E. Brown, *The Epistles of John* (Garden City, N.Y.: Doubleday, 1982), 503.

26. Ibid., 496. Some interpreters take this apocalyptic, eschatological literature and try to wed it to a particular historical context. For instance, the idea of a "spirit of Antichrist" has been made a figure in the schemes of biblical literalists.

27. Ibid., 505.

28. The language of "Spirit" and "spirits" is hard to delineate in this passage. At least we can distinguish between divine and human spirits; however, human spirit that makes right confession is also of God.

29. Christopher Morse, *Not Every Spirit: A Dogmatics of Christian Disbelief* (Valley Forge, Pa.: Trinity Press International, 1994), 181.

30. Frank Rogers Jr., "Discernment," in *Practicing Our Faith: A Way of*

Life for a Searching People, ed. Dorothy C. Bass (San Francisco: Jossey-Bass, 1997), 113.

31. Morse, *Not Every Spirit*, 5.

32. See Danny E. Morris and Charles M. Olsen, *Discerning God's Will Together: A Spiritual Practice for the Church* (Nashville: Upper Room Books, 1997). See also Thomas Green, *Weeds Among the Wheat* (Notre Dame, Ind.: Ave Maria Press, 1984) and Casiano Floristan and Christian Duquoc, eds., *Discernment of the Spirit and of Spirits* (New York: Seabury, 1979).

33. Morris and Olsen, *Discerning God's Will Together*, 63.

34. Among the spiritual classics, *The Spiritual Exercises of St. Ignatius*, *The Imitation of Christ* by St. Thomas à Kempis and the *Dialogue of St. Catherine of Siena* devote considerable attention to the issue of spiritual discernment.

35. Frank Rogers ("Discernment," 114–116) offers six normative (though not exhaustive) criteria to guide the communal practice of discernment: (1) fidelity to Scripture and the tradition; (2) fruit of the Spirit; (3) inner authority and peace; (4) communal harmony; (5) enhancement rather than extinction of life; and (6) integrity in the process of discernment.

36. Luke Timothy Johnson, *Scripture and Discernment: Decision Making in the Church* (Nashville: Abingdon, 1996), 109.

37. In 1 Corinthians 14:29, Paul calls for persons to weigh what the prophets have said in the assembly. Presumably, he is asking those so gifted to exercise their discernment on behalf of the congregation.

38. Johnson points to the signal importance of this text, because it "gives the fullest picture in the New Testament of the process by which the church reaches decision" (*Scripture and Discernment*, 78).

39. This description comes from John V. Taylor, *The Go-Between God: The Holy Spirit and the Christian Mission* (New York: Oxford University Press, 1972), 18.

40. Cf. Job 21:18: "How often are [the wicked] like straw before the wind, and like chaff that the storm carries away?" An image frequently in Scripture is that of *ruach* separating good persons from evil persons.

41. Lee E. Snook, *What in the World Is God Doing? Re-imagining Spirit and Power* (Minneapolis: Fortress, 1999), 93.

42. Tonghou Ngong David, "Left Behind," *Theology Today* 59, no. 2 (July 2002): 285. Mr. David is a student at Central Baptist Theological Seminary.

43. Dr. Gustavo Paràjon, a distinguished American Baptist missionary in Nicaragua, has been recognized by the government for his groundbreaking work in providing health care for outlying communities.

44. Though a decade old now, Cornel West's *Race Matters* (Boston: Beacon Press, 1993) perceptively interprets the politics of race as well as the nihilism in black America.

45. In his trilogy, *The Powers*, Walter Wink has made a stellar contribution

to contemporary understanding of the biblical language of "powers and prin-cipalities," the archons of this age. The basic interpretative material is laid out in the first volume, *Naming the Powers: The Language of Power in the New Testament* (Philadelphia: Westminster, 1984), 104–118.

46. See the analysis by Barbara Brown Zikmund, "Feminist Consciousness in Historical Perspective," in *Feminist Interpretation of the Bible*, ed. Letty M. Russell (Philadelphia: Westminster, 1985), 21–29.

47. See the overview by Carolyn De Swarte Gifford, "Women in Social Reform Movements," in *Women and Religion in America*, Vol. 1, ed. Rosemary Radford Ruether and Rosemary Skinner Keller (San Francisco: Harper & Row, 1981), 294–303.

48. Martin Luther King Jr., *Stride Toward Freedom* (New York: Harper & Row, 1958), 107.

49. Kenneth L. Smith and Ira G. Zepp Jr., *Search for the Beloved Community: The Thinking of Martin Luther King, Jr.* (Valley Forge, Pa.: Judson Press, 1988), 60.

50. Her story is recounted by Olive Gilbert, *Narrative of Sojourner Truth* (Boston: 1875).

51. See Emilie M. Townes, ed., *Embracing the Spirit: Womanist Perspectives on Hope, Salvation, and Transformation* (Maryknoll, N.Y.: Orbis, 1997), for an excellent anthology that explores the many streams of religious and cultur-al life that the Spirit is empowering women to navigate.

52. E. Glenn Hinson uses this description to identify persons with capacities and vision that transcend their particular epoch.

53. Snook, *What in the World?*, 100.

54. Ibid., 101.

55. Nicholas M. Healy, *Church, World and the Christian Life: Practical-Prophetic Ecclesiology* (Cambridge: Cambridge University Press, 2000), 69.

56. See 1 Corinthians 12:22-26 for Paul's articulation of the need for care for all the members of the body, especially the weak.

57. Moltmann, *The Spirit of Life*, 244.

58. Peter C. Hodgson, *Winds of the Spirit: A Constructive Christian Theology* (Louisville: Westminster John Knox, 1994), 291.

59. These images are drawn from Henry Alford's 1844 hymn text, "Come, Ye Thankful People, Come."

CHAPTER 8

HONORING FAITH'S PROMISE

My dwelling place shall be with them; and I will
be their God, and they shall be my people.
—Ezekiel 37:27

If the Spirit of [the One] who raised Jesus from
the dead dwells in you, [the One] who raised Christ
from the dead will give life to your mortal bodies also
through [the] Spirit [who] dwells in you.
—Romans 8:11

The creation itself will be set free from its bondage to decay
and will obtain the freedom of the glory of the children of God.
—Romans 8:21

OUR STUDY HAS EXPLORED THE BREADTH OF THE SPIRIT'S MOVEMENT
in the life of God and the life of the world. We have discovered
that Spirit cannot be contained by creed or church or even the
Christ. Spirit is larger, more universal than we can imagine, yet
is particular and unique as God's presence with us. In the preceding chapter we looked at the winnowing work of Spirit, gifting and guiding. We also looked at Spirit as God's power to
"disrupt the social hierarchy in order to engender healing and
renewal among the victimized and disadvantaged."[1] Ever present, ever going before us, the Spirit's work is not yet completed. What vision of consummation can sustain our labor now
and offer reassurance for the future? What remains for the
Spirit to accomplish?

These questions prompt us to examine the ways in which the Spirit honors faith's promise in liberating, recreating, and consummating all created reality, whose life is brought to fullness in God. Key metaphors for the consummation of all creation include "faith becoming sight," "the lion and the lamb lying down together," "making war nor more," "a new heaven and a new earth," "sitting at table with those from east and west," "a little child leading them," "the healing of the nations," and many other visually inviting portrayals. Faith clings to these as narrated promise in Scripture,[2] and the Spirit enlivens hope toward their realization.

Eschatology is, I must confess, the area in which I struggle the most in teaching theology. Usually there is too little time at the end of the semester to give this doctrine in theology its due, and the provisionality of our affirmations gives us pause. In the past I have trivialized the significance of this topic by giving a fake objective exam that identified the millennium as a "bug with a thousand legs," the "New Jerusalem" as a china pattern popularized by Golda Meier, and the "great tribulation" as a semester in my feminist theology course.[3] I have repented of these foibles committed in the adolescence of my professorship. Eschatology should not be taken so lightly, nor should it be treated as one topic amidst the other topics of constructive theology, for all of theology is eschatological in orientation.[4]

Eschatology has been too much the purview of cranks, and those of us who live in some reaction to the exaggerated certitude of the dispensationalists, the chart makers, the calculations of the Hal Lindseys, or the fiction of the Tim LaHayes err by saying too little rather than too much.[5] Liberalism has been characterized by its accentuation of this world and agnosticism about any "world to come." This has led to great emphases on social justice, liberative movements, and activism in resisting the powers. It has also led to resignation or despair when we do not see "the mighty cast down" and "the hungry filled with good things" (Luke 1:52-53).

Whereas earlier generations might have been more interested in the specifics of eschatological thinking, ours is marked more by hopeless skepticism that the earth's ills will ever be put right. Proclaiming any continuity between this world and the next seems even more improbable.

Another critical issue is the relation of time and eternity.[6] How do we conceive of God working through time, yet acknowledge that time is bounded by God's eternal presence, both before and after creation as we know it? Clearly, God deigns to work through the finitude of time, as demonstrated through the history of creation and human civilization, but these are not of themselves eternal. Obviously, to speak in this way also suggests that space likewise is finite. God has given both time and space for creation to flourish, but they are not eternal. They too must be transformed by the Spirit in order to participate in God's glory.

Traditionally, eschatology has been approached from the perspective of the return of Christ, the destiny of the unevangelized (i.e., non-Christians), the resurrection of the dead, the hope of glory for the redeemed, the earth's demise, the "great white throne" where the supreme judge sits (Revelation 20:11), judgment with regard to inclusion and exclusion (not to mention rewards), and so on. This approach has proved unsatisfactory not only because of the density of the apocalyptic language of Scripture, but also because it all seems to be an inbreaking from beyond rather than a continuity with what is already occurring in this world. There is also a glaring omission: the Spirit does not figure clearly in this interpretive framework, unlike the other two members of the Trinity.

I believe that it is necessary to look further into the extent of the Spirit's work in the summing up of all things, honoring faith's promise. The beginning of Scripture shows the Spirit's work in bringing forth life, and at the end of Scripture, the Spirit is still working on making "all things new," which refers to this same world. As Elizabeth Johnson contends, "When creation is seen together with its future of liberation in God, any residual dualism or overspiritu-alizing regarding the scope of the Spirit's agency is put to rest."[7] We do not examine the Spirit as an abstract idea, but through our earth-centered understanding. Although not exhaustive, this form of pneumatological reflection at least keeps us from nonbiblical meta-physical speculation, which evokes little interest in what Jürgen Moltmann calls the "ecology of the creative Spirit."[8] As we have seen, the Bible characterizes Spirit as God's movement toward and in creation; moreover, this loving attentiveness is not yet spent.

The Spirit as life-giver, healer, and sustainer continues the Trinitarian project with creation to its ultimate realization. Thus, comments Moltmann, "It is pneumatology that brings Christology and eschatology together."[9] This is particularly true when we regard resurrection as the paradigm for all creation. To that we turn to the major focus of this chapter: rising with Christ and con-summating creation. Then more briefly we will ask about the inclusion of those who have not come to God in the *ordo salutis* of Christianity, yet hope toward God. As a final movement, we will envision the ultimate filling with presence, the realization of the epi-clesis, when God invites all into the richness of the divine life,[10] welcoming all into the eternal perichoretic dance of ecstasy.

RISING WITH CHRIST

Resurrection occurs in the power of the Spirit. The resurrection of Christ, the resurrection of Christians, and the resurrection of cre-ation are expressions of the Spirit, who is supremely the giver of new life. As we noted in chapter 4, the church has not sufficiently utilized the wide-ranging scriptural witness to resurrection, but has tended to treat the rising of Christ in a manner that disconnects his resurrection with our own hope of life beyond death and shows little interest in the destiny of the universe. Certainly I am not suggesting that resurrection of the Crucified One can be overemphasized; however, I do believe that treating it in isolation from other creaturely beings limits the significance of God's holistic resurrecting movement. Thus, we need to examine two aspects of resurrection: (1) how the Spirit resurrects the individual within community for eternal life, and (2) how all creation participates in the resurrection of the Christ by the life-giving Spirit.

Recently, theologians in the West have reawakened to the significance of the community for theological understanding.[11] The long shadow of Descartes, with its preoccupying focus on the significance of the individual, has lingered. Remember, he said "I," not "we." This "turn to the subject" characteristic of Enlightenment philosophers and theologians has shaped much theological thinking about the future into an exclusively "personal eschatology." This is understandable to some degree because death is the culminating event of an individual's life, and it is borne alone in certain respects, yet the communal dimensions of resurrection have been neglected. Indeed, many pastoral concerns when interpreting death revolve around questions of continued personal identity, recognition of loved ones gone before, and how close earthly relations will or will not endure. Caroline Walker Bynum's analysis of current philosophical discourse and of contemporary popular culture underscores this concern for ongoing, individual, embodied identity. She writes,

> Americans, like medieval poets and theologians, consider any survival that really counts to entail the survival of body....Movies such as *Maxie, Chances Are, Robocop, Total Recall, Switch, Freejack,* and *Death Becomes Her* gross millions; their drama lies in the suggestion that 'I' am not 'I' unless my body, with all it implies (sex and sexual orientation, race, temperament, etc.), survives.[12]

Resurrected life does not sound any different from life now, according to this description. In addition, this vision seems to

143

presume that spirit is something that creatures possess by permanent right. To be alive (in this life or the next), however, is "to be in receipt of that life from God,"[13] as Gary Badcock rightly interprets Scripture.

Can we learn to speak of the resurrection of the body of Christ in such a way as to preserve its character as gift and gather up the dismembering impulses that individualize resurrection? Further, how can we imagine a different kind of existence, both continuous and discontinuous with life as we know it? The apostolic witness remains formative for our faith.

The seed is the oldest Christian metaphor for the resurrection of the body. It is the dominant metaphor in the text that, more than any other, has guided discussion of the resurrection: 1 Corinthians 15.

> But someone will ask, "How are the dead raised? With what kind of body do they come?" Fool! What you sow does not come to life unless it dies. And as for what you sow, you do not sow the body that is to be, but a bare seed, perhaps of wheat or of some other grain. But God gives it a body as he has chosen, and to each kind of seed its own body. (1 Corinthians 15:35-38)

In early interpretation this Pauline text was often glossed with John 12:24: "Very truly, I tell you, unless a grain of wheat falls into the earth and dies, it remains just a single grain; but if it dies, it bears much fruit."

The first text speaks of a corporate harvest; the second text points to the impending death of Jesus, who as a "solitary seed" does not remain alone, but is joined by a great company. The logic seems obvious: no one plants a single seed. The death of Jesus precedes our own, but is not separated from it. The New Testament makes the resurrection of Jesus normative, the one through whom "all are made alive" (1 Corinthians 15:22). Thus, the resurrection of Jesus is spoken of in the language of "first fruits"; he is, in the words of John A. T. Robinson, a "genuine sample of the whole."[14] Our confession is that Jesus, who has proleptically gone before us, makes the general resurrection "at the last day" a reliable prospect.

Another distinctive accent found in the Pauline writings suggests that our resurrection has already begun through baptism. Further, because we have in the spiritual sense passed from death into life, the Spirit grants us assurance[15] through indwelling us that we will be sustained through physical death, as was Jesus. "Therefore we have been buried with him by baptism into death, so that, just as Christ was raised from the dead by the glory of [God], so we too might walk in newness of life" (Romans 6:4).

> But you are not in the flesh; you are in the Spirit, since the Spirit of God dwells in you. Anyone who does not have the Spirit of Christ does not belong to him. But if Christ is in you, though the body is dead because of sin, the Spirit is life because of righteousness. If the Spirit of [the One] who raised Jesus from the dead dwells in you, [the One] who raised Christ from the dead will give life to your mortal bodies also through [the] Spirit, [who] dwells in you. (Romans 8:9-11)

Thus, resurrection is the rebirth of embodied persons, and it begins in this life. Although we are being transformed, we remain distinctively ourselves within the community of Christ's members.

We must not miss the interplay between the body of Christ and bodies in these and other Pauline texts about resurrection. The body of Christ is best understood as an organic, corporate expression of resurrection life. Our bodies (our whole selves) are incorporated into the death and resurrection of Jesus Christ through Christian initiation, which tells the deepest truth about our lives. The Spirit moves in the birth water of our baptism, that we might be born anew "to a living hope" as Christ's continuing enfleshment in the world. Moltmann describes the proleptic work of the Spirit in realizing eschatological hope in the present: "If according to the Christian hope 'the transfiguration of the body' consists of the raising from death to eternal life, then it is already experienced here and now in the Spirit of life, which interpenetrates body and soul and wakens all our vital powers. Eternal love transfigures the body."[16]

And we are the body of Christ, and individually "membranes thereof" (1 Corinthians 12:27), as Robinson translates it.[17] Resurrection of the body encompasses the whole community.[18] Peter Hodgson well understands this corporate emphasis. In his words, resurrection means "taking up an action or function by which one's identity is preserved in a new kind of communal, corporate embodiment that is spiritual in character....The spiritual body is a spiritual community, a community created by the Spirit."[19]

In her study of interpretations of resurrection in historical theology, Bynum observes, "Whatever else the doctrine of universal resurrection has been said to reveal, those who refer to it always use it to underline the extraordinary power necessary to create and recreate."[20] It is the extraordinary power of the Spirit who fits us for eternal life—our continuing life is because God continues to vivify us with God's own breath. It is the power of the Spirit who makes possible being "born from above" (John 3:3,7).[21] It is the power of the Spirit who incorporates us into Christ, who has triumphed over death.

Resurrection in the body of Christ gives meaning to human history, giving it a unifying, coherent trajectory. Is history going somewhere? Not as an abstraction subject to blind fate, but as a human reality bounded by the Spirit of God, it is. Once again I turn to Johnson's words: "The Spirit's renewing power thus manifests itself historically in shaping the praxis of freedom, those myriad forms of peoples' struggle toward more peaceful and equitable circumstances, a stunning example being women's struggle against sexism."[22] She describes the Spirit's liberative action further: "In the biblical prophetic tradition the Spirit's presence is consistently linked with the power to denounce social wrongdoing, announce comfort for those who are suffering, and bring about justice for the poor."[23] The cruel powers and principalities, the despotic rulers and structures, will not have the last word. Resurrection also can describe the rising up of people to protest their oppression. When they stand up, straightening their backs and strengthening their resolve to live in freedom, they presage the ultimate liberation promised by the Spirit.[24]

CONSUMMATING CREATION

Resurrection concerns not just humanity, but all creation. Creation is more than a theatrical backdrop for the human "stars" of the production. According to George Maloney, it is the continuing refrain of the Bible that the whole world will reach its completion "in being transfigured from its deformity, its 'vanity' as Paul calls it, into a 'renovated creation.' Our world will not be annihilated, but transfigured."[25]

God as Spirit will not let the beloved creation pass away into nothingness, but will renew it through death into life, that it might share in what it eagerly longs for: the glorious freedom of the children of God. Hodgson refers to this work of the Spirit as the "liberation of the world." By this description, he gathers up the whole process "of the return of the world from alienated otherness and separateness to its end in the divine life."[26] The vanity or futility of all of creation is grounded in its finitude, its mortality and death; this reality is exacerbated by the sinful machinations of humanity. However, because God subjected it in hope (Romans 8:20) to its groaning process of self-realization, God can liberate it. The Spirit, then, "is the transformer of futility into freedom,"[27] as Romans 8 anticipates. This freedom entails the overcoming of destruction, bondage, and lack of fruition.

The Spirit does not work alone in this, however. Elizabeth Johnson wisely insists that the resurrection of all creation is a collaborative divine and human enterprise:

> Like a midwife she [the Spirit] works deftly with those in pain and struggle to bring about the new creation (Ps 22:9-10). Through the mediation of human praxis she comes to wash what is unclean; pour water upon what is arid; heal what is hurt; make flexible what is rigid; warm what is freezing; straighten out what is crooked and bent.[28]

Without the Spirit, we would not have an eschatological orientation that allows us to live in hope and work toward transformation.

In Moltmann's view, the vulnerable nearness of God as abiding Spirit "awakens new and hitherto unsuspected expectations about life. The experience of the Spirit is the reason for the eschatological longing for the completion of salvation, the redemption of the body and the new creation of all things."[29] The Spirit allows us to know that we are not yet finished, nor is the glory of God fully expressed in this groaning world. Moltmann continues, "It is the experience of the Spirit which makes Christians in every society restless and homeless, and on the search for the kingdom of God (Heb. 13:14), for it is this experience of God which makes them controvert and contravene a godless world of violence and death."[30]

It is only because of the Spirit that this world can move through dying to living; the all-awakening, all-resurrecting, all-sustaining Spirit of God, in the words of Anne Primavesi, "enables each species to be what it is intended to be within the ecosystem which surrounds it, and is the source of newness and diversity in each species through the action and interaction of others."[31] Her description applies to the Spirit's work in creation both now and in the future. All will be gathered up in the Spirit's recreation of the cosmos. Through death will come new life; resurrection allows the Easter spring for all creation. It is the true pattern, the Christic pattern, of the tissue of life—dying and rising.

Such wide affirmation offers comfort and hope to those who grieve the loss not only of fellow human beings, but also of those loving animal friends that have made their lives more joyful and connected to the pneumatic creation. When our beloved Martin Luther Marshall-Green, a theologically attentive schnauzer, died at the age of fourteen, I realized that I longed for more than the schnauzer species to continue in the life beyond; I wanted the schnauzer whose eyes and bark I knew so well to be a part of the Spirit's consummating gift. I trust that Luther (the schnauzer) is keeping good company already, or at least is held by the power of God, along with all creation, while awaiting freedom from bondage to decay (Romans 8:21).

Creation has its own time and space within God's providence; God let it be and did not overwhelm it with the heaviness of divine presence. The "primordial self-restriction of God (*tzimtzum*)"[32] that allows God to share agency in the world will end when all creation is filled with the knowledge of the glory of God (Numbers 14:21; Habakkuk 2:14).

Perhaps it is easier to articulate the universal conviction that all creation shares in the resurrection power of the Spirit than to express the particular hopes of persons whose pathway is not informed by the biblical story. In what way does their faith hold promise within the vivifying work of God's Spirit?

HOPING TOWARD GOD

An increase in religious tolerance (at least in many sectors) and a growing receptivity to pluralism in contemporary society have opened avenues of dialogue never before possible between religions. As one learns more about other religious pathways, one discovers not only momentous differences, but also striking similarities of meaning. At this point in human history, we must find new ways to engage adherents of the disparate religions for the sake of understanding and for the sake of continued coexistence. Rowan Williams warns against using other people "as symbols for points on your map, values in your scheme of things. When you get used to imposing meanings in this way, you silence the stranger's account of who they are; and that can mean both metaphorical and literal death."[33] Although our missionary forebears may have thought that if persons simply hear the proclamation of the gospel, they will want to convert to Christianity, that assumption is no longer reliable. Many resist Christian faith because of its cultural affiliation with Europe and North America, and thereby discount its relevance for their contexts.[34] Religious traditions are living, emerging realities that show little sign of dissipating.

Throughout Christian history, compassionate persons have sought to understand the hopes of persons who follow other ways of faith. Because inclusion in the life eternal usually has been framed with reference to one's confession of the lordship of Christ, what can be said of those whose historical, geographical, and cultural experience has led them to cling to their indigenous way of faith, perhaps without knowledge of the claims concerning Jesus Christ, or either ignoring or actively resisting them?

When we can cease our triumphalist monologue long enough to listen deeply, we can hear the breathing of the Spirit through these other ways of faith. It seems plausible to interpret the truth that is encountered as nothing less than the work of God's Spirit guiding into all truth (John 16:13). Long ago, St. Irenaeus addressed this problem when he wrote, "There is but one and the same God who, from the beginning to the end by various dispensations, comes to the rescue of humankind."[35] What is the mode of God's activity in traditions other than the Christian?

Often, we have sought to address this theological issue by resort to a cosmic Christology, which ends up making others "anonymous Christians"[36] or offers a postmortem encounter with the living Christ, toward whom they had yearned in an unthematized manner.[37] The Christocentrism of this approach, reminiscent of Barth, threatens to eclipse a pneumatological avenue that recognizes God already at work in other ways of faith.

The Spirit is universally present in the world, bringing awareness of the ways of God to all persons of faith. Furthermore, the Spirit stirs hope among those who would deny having religious faith in the traditional sense. No one eludes the Spirit's searching, awakening, drawing presence. The Spirit remains unrequited as long as those whom God loves move away from the relationship for which they were created. John Taylor observes that as "citizens of a forgiven universe,"[38] all people have access to the Spirit, who works "in all ages and all cultures,"[39] evoking response to the fullness of God.[40] Because on Good Friday, God has issued a general pardon to the whole world,[41] the pouring out of Spirit is unceasing, flowing unchecked into all the streams of faith in the world.

Thus, we may agree with the perspective of John McIntyre, who writes,

> The Holy Spirit is with them guiding and directing them Godwards, and making sure for them the uncovenanted mercies of that God. Might we also add that the beliefs and works of the people of other faiths are the expression of that presence of the Spirit with them?...I would hang on to the conviction that they have not wandered beyond the mercy of God or the compassion of his spirit.[42]

Johnson sounds even more positive about the Spirit-prompted expression of faith inhering in other religious traditions:

> As the experience of finding wholeness and meaning comes to expression in diverse cultures and ages, the panoply of the world's religious traditions takes shape. No people are devoid of the inspiration of the Spirit. In ways know only to herself, she orients human beings toward ultimate mystery and the fullness of coming blessing through movements of their conscience and rays of goodness and truth found in their diverse religious communities.[43]

It is because the Spirit is at work in traditions beyond the Christian one that we may share in humility the truth we have come to know; the Spirit makes possible a coordinated hope with other peoples of God. Does this vision diminish the significance of the Christ? Not at all. Actually, it expands the force field of the Spirit in which persons encounter resurrection life, which emanates from the risen Christ.

Finally, this is the point in the construction at which to note the interface of the Spirit's work with the risen Christ. One cannot seek God without seeking the sender of Jesus Christ; one cannot follow the Spirit's guidance without ultimately encountering the source from whom the Spirit proceeds and the Christ whose witness the Spirit extends. The reciprocal work of the Spirit and the Christ continues as the Spirit bears witness to God's redeeming grace in Jesus, and the Christ gives the Spirit freely to those who seek God. The Trinitarian movement throughout the world thus creates access for varying perspectives to enter into the divine life now, or in God's further transfiguring work. In fact, we cannot dismember the Trinity, but must regard it as a "reality that is so mutually self-participative that distinctions can no longer be drawn,"[44] as David Cunningham rightly argues.

Thus, the Spirit labors to honor faith's promise, albeit in its different forms and practices that characterize the religious diversity of our time. And as the Spirit draws persons to God, they are moving toward the one we confess as Trinity. Although we cannot say with certainty how their faith is met by the grace of God, the Spirit's sustaining presence with them grants hope.

FILLING WITH PRESENCE

Fullness, overspilling plenitude, and the social and ecological justice intrinsic to Scripture's proclamation of the end-time Sabbath[45] are key dimensions of the Spirit's crafting of consummation. In this study, we are moving toward a view of resurrection as eternal *perichoresis* in God. The teleology of creation is that "God might be all in all." The goal of resurrection now comes into view: God has opened a space in the divine life in which all the living participate, suffused with the glory of God. Toward the end of *The Trinity and the Kingdom*, Moltmann offers a description of this indwelling: "If through the experience of the Spirit men and women in their physical nature become God's temple (I Cor. 6.13bff.), then they are anticipating the glory in which the whole world will become the temple of the triune God (Rev. 21.3)."[46]

What we experience in promissory grace now, we will experience in the fullness of eschatological restoration. Throughout this study, I have drawn from the Cappadocian theologians, who envisioned the Trinity dwelling in the richness of community. The mutual indwelling allows the divine "persons" to be defined through their relations with one another. The unceasing movement of ecstasy in which persons are literally constituted by standing outside of themselves in self-emptying for the other forms the paradigm for the dance of creation as it joins the dynamism of the eternal One. Giving and receiving life, the engendering Spirit ultimately will fill all with the fullness of God. This is never an exclusive circle, however, for the Spirit makes space for us that we may enter into the unity and communion within the being of God.

I see this truth as I behold my favorite icon, Andrei Rublev's The Holy Trinity, which hangs above the desk in my office. Over the years, as I have prayed before it and meditated on its depiction of communion, I have felt the pull of the Spirit drawing me into the Trinitarian hospitality it portrays. Although the three figures lean toward one another in love and attentiveness, there is an open space. It is as if the beholder is invited to pull up a chair to the nearside of the table in the foreground and enter the intimate conversation.[47]

God in humility has so bound the divine being to human being (and all creation) that God's being "is completed by the return of all things to God."[48] Created life is brought to full flourishing by the welcome of the hospitable Spiritual Presence. It is the Spirit's role ever to connect creaturely being with divine being, making all present to one another.

In eschatological hope we pray, *Veni Creator Spiritus*: Come, Holy Spirit, renew the whole of creation. In every time and place, the church requires what Yves Congar calls "one long epiclesis,"[49] a continual invocation of the Spirit to inspire its forms. Christian faith contends that the church is the focused representation of resurrection life; it serves as an anticipatory sign and sacrament of the new humanity, guiding all creation to its consummation.

The church also cries for the Spirit of life to honor faith's promise. It is not diminished by spiritual life *extra ecclesiam*, but rejoices that the Spirit cannot be contained by its conventions. Indwelling presence is the work of the Holy Spirit. The gifts of God in throbbing creation, the bestowal of God's own self in Jesus, baptism that plunges us into the life of Christ, sharing in resurrection life, the communion of the saints, and the life everlasting—all these come to realization in the power of new life, the Spirit of God.

NOTES

1. Mark Wallace, *Fragments of the Spirit: Nature, Violence, and the Renewal of Creation* (New York: Continuum, 1996), 211–212.

2. See Ronald F. Thiemann, *Revelation and Theology: The Gospel as Narrated Promise* (Notre Dame, Ind.: University of Notre Dame Press, 1985).

3. I also wryly suggested that the rapture would be difficult for those over-weight as motivation to help students and professor get better in shape.

4. The early Christian conviction was that the eschaton, the last or ultimate period, had been inaugurated through the ministry and resurrection of Jesus. Although this period was not yet fully realized, many signs indicated this inbreaking of the future: the resurrection of the dead, the outpouring of the Spirit, the coming of God's reign, and the overcoming of the powers of evil. Many twentieth-century theologians have attempted to recapture this eschato-logical orientation, among them Karl Barth and Rudolf Bultmann, and more recently, Jürgen Moltmann and Wolfhart Pannenberg.

5. As the twentieth century closed and this new millennium began, a renew-al of speculation about the winding up of human history has occurred, espe-cially with heightened fear of terrorism, ecological disaster, and global warfare. Given the propensity of some "end time" biblical interpreters to look for "signs," it is important to consider eschatology as that which "lasts" rather than what which "comes last" (some so-called proof that the end is near) on the historical plane.

6. In Jürgen Moltmann's eschatology, time ends in the eternity of God. See Moltmann's *The Coming of God: Christian Eschatology* (Minneapolis: Fortress, 1996), 279–295.

7. Elizabeth A. Johnson, *She Who Is: The Mystery of God in Feminist Theological Discourse* (New York: Crossroad, 1992), 138.

8. Jürgen Moltmann, *The Source of Life: The Holy Spirit and the Theology of Life,* trans. Margaret Kohl (Minneapolis: Fortress, 1997), 111.

9. Jürgen Moltmann, *The Spirit of Life: A Universal Affirmation,* trans. Margaret Kohl (Minneapolis: Fortress, 1992), 69.

10. Robert W. Jenson calls this event the "Great Transformation," our entry into the life of the triune God. See his essay "The Great Transformation," in *The Last Things: Biblical and Theological Perspectives on Eschatology,* ed. Carl E. Braaten and Robert W. Jenson (Grand Rapids: Eerdmans, 2002), 35–36.

11. Miroslav Volf's *After Our Likeness: The Church as the Image of the Trinity* (Grand Rapids: Eerdmans, 1998) examines the communal ground of ecclesial identity in the divine communion of the Trinity. This particular empha-sis in contemporary theology is replacing the well-worn and problematic accen-tuation of individualism. See also George Rupp's *Commitment and*

Community (Minneapolis: Fortress, 1989), an analysis of the significant role of community in public life and in the context of religious pluralism.

12. Caroline Walker Bynum, The Resurrection of the Body in Western Christianity, 200–1336 (New York: Columbia University Press, 1995), 15.

13. Gary A. Badcock, Light of Truth and Fire of Love: A Theology of the Holy Spirit (Grand Rapids: Eerdmans, 1997), 10.

14. John A. T. Robinson, The Human Face of God (London: SCM, 1973), 140.

15. Paul calls it the "first installment" or "deposit"; the Spirit's indwelling is the "guarantee" (2 Corinthians 1:22; 5:5).

16. Moltmann, The Spirit of Life, 95.

17. John A. T. Robinson, The Body: A Study in Pauline Theology (Philadelphia: Westminster, 1952), 51.

18. Rudolf Bultmann and John A. T. Robinson argued that the Pauline sōma could be read as "community"—a rendering never sufficiently explored, in my judgment.

19. Peter C. Hodgson, Winds of the Spirit: A Constructive Christian Theology (Louisville: Westminster John Knox, 1994), 329–330.

20. Bynum, Resurrection of the Body, 2.

21. The KJV has "born again." The NRSV has "born from above," which sustains the particular spatial language of the Fourth Gospel.

22. Johnson, She Who Is, 137.

23. Ibid., 136.

24. In The Source of Life, Moltmann describes three postures of prayer: prostration, kneeling, and standing. Whereas the first two describe absolute subservience and profound humility, respectively, the third welcomes the Holy Spirit. "It is an attitude of a great expectation and loving readiness to receive and embrace. The people who in this posture open themselves for God are free men and women" (128).

25. George A. Maloney, The Spirit Broods Over the World (New York: Alba House, 1993), 158.

26. Hodgson, Winds of the Spirit, 291–292.

27. Ibid., 320.

28. Johnson, She Who Is, 136.

29. Moltmann, The Spirit of Life, 73.

30. Ibid.

31. Anne Primavesi, From Apocalypse to Genesis: Ecology, Feminism and Christianity (Minneapolis: Fortress, 1991), 262.

32. Moltmann, The Coming of God, 297.

33. Rowan Williams, Writing in the Dust: After September 11 (Grand Rapids: Eerdmans, 2002), 64. Williams is warning about the ways Christians historically have caricatured other faiths to buttress their own thinking; in our day, he cautions Christians about their relationships with Muslims, for much is at stake.

34. The exception to this is the "global South" (especially Africa and South America), which currently is the scene of great expansion in Christianity. See Sara Miller, "Global Gospel," *Christian Century*, Vol. 119, No. 15 (July 17, 2002): 20–27.

35. *Against Heresies* 3.12.13, as cited by Elizabeth Johnson, *She Who Is*, 139.

36. Karl Rahner coined this description, which has been met with a welter of responses. See, among his many works that address this issue, "Anonymous Christians," in *Theological Investigations*, vol. 6, trans. K. H. Kruger and B. Kruger (Baltimore: Helicon, 1969), 390–398.

37. See the publication of my doctoral dissertation, *No Salvation Outside the Church? A Critical Inquiry* (Lewiston: Edwin Mellen, 1993). Since the writing of that study, I have become much more explicitly trinitarian in my theological construction, making me less christomonistic in thinking about other ways of faith. While my soteriology is still firmly anchored in Christology, the reciprocity of Spirit and Christ opens new possibilities for faith in God to converge within God's trinitarian expression of mission.

38. John V. Taylor, *The Go-Between God: The Holy Spirit and the Christian Mission* (Philadelphia: Fortress, 1973), 180.

39. Ibid., 191.

40. Mark Heim speaks of "salvations" when referring to the varied ways that religious traditions hope in God. Their vision of the summing up of human history depends upon a different set of expectations. His Christian perspective on religious diversity is articulated in *Salvations: Truth and Difference in Religion* (Maryknoll, N.Y.: Orbis, 1995), esp. 158–171.

41. Moltmann, *The Coming of God*, 254.

42. John McIntyre, *The Shape of Pneumatology: Studies in the Doctrine of the Holy Spirit* (Edinburgh: Clark, 1997), 288–289.

43. Johnson, *She Who Is*, 139.

44. David S. Cunningham, *These Three Are One: The Practice of Trinitarian Theology* (London: Blackwell, 1998), 178.

45. Moltmann, *The Spirit of Life*, 73.

46. Jürgen Moltmann, *The Trinity and the Kingdom: The Doctrine of God*, trans. Margaret Kohl (San Francisco: Harper & Row, 1981), 212.

47. I have learned about this icon through reading Henri Nouwen's *Behold the Beauty of the Lord: Praying with Icons* (Notre Dame, Ind.: Ave Maria Press, 1987).

48. Hodgson, *Winds of the Spirit*, 170.

49. Yves Congar, *I Believe in the Holy Spirit*, vol. 3, trans. David Smith (New York: Seabury, 1983), 267–272.

CHAPTER 9

PARTICIPATING IN THE LIFE OF GOD

Do you not know that your
body is a temple of the Holy Spirit
within you, which you have from God,
and that you are not your own?
—1 Corinthians 6:19

Your life is hidden with Christ in God.
—Colossians 3:3

[God] will dwell with them as their God; they will
be [God's] people, and [God] will be with them.
—Revelation 21:3

THE PRIMARY METAPHOR WOVEN THROUGHOUT THIS STUDY IS THE idea that the Spirit is inviting all creation to join in the dance that characterizes God's life. The Spirit as God's inexhaustible, dancing power creates an ongoing movement between divine and creaturely being. Because the *perichoresis* of God is open for the participation of all creation, all find identity through this overarching rhythm of life. Of human participants in this dance, Jürgen Moltmann writes, "People who are moved by God's Spirit move themselves, and people who experience grace move gracefully."[1]

Dance is always a work of multiple contributors. Describing it in concrete terms, it is comprised of space, rhythm, music, steps (ordered or improvised), breath, touch, embrace, parallel or contrasting movements, and partners. Dancing may include all these factors, yet it is a living reality that, when performed, is larger than the aggregate of factors—a synergism that creates something new. It is analogous to the reflection of the philosophers who suggest that we do not so much play games as games play us. The throbbing dance of the universe, which the Spirit invites all to join, compels the participants to express most fully their true identity as they dance their praise of God, with God.

The texts that form the epigraph for this concluding chapter offer images of a sanctuary or tabernacle, a reciprocal indwelling of human and divine, another way to think about *perichoresis*. These pictures of habitation in which persons are the temple of the Spirit, or God tabernacles within the people of God, offer insight into the intimate ways we share life with God in mutual participation.

It is by the Spirit that we participate in the life of God and God participates in our life together. As we have noted, in Scripture the Spirit is often linked to communion (*koinōnia*). I prefer to translate the word as "participation," which suggests that we indwell and are indwelt by the lives of others. This is true of our relation with God and with one another. It is a Trinitarian virtue to live life opened out in relationality.[2]

We have sought to think deeply about the Holy Spirit, aware that it is a "bewildering, tearing exercise."[3] We have sought to recover the centrality of Trinitarian pneumatology in constructive theology, believing that this approach, shaped by the wisdom of early Christian teachers, can helpfully address many contemporary concerns. Although I have not treated the issue of the feminine character of the Spirit,[4] because that tends to masculinize the other persons of the triune God in a distorting manner, I have chosen to make pneumatology the door through which to consider the being of God. This approach does have the benefit of subverting "the dominance of the patriarchal image of God so detrimental to the mystery of God and the well-being of human community."5 Furthermore, the approach of these chapters has deliberately bracketed most of the soteriological concerns because, in my judgment, too much emphasis has been given to the convicting power of the Spirit rather than the creative power.

I also have sought to make the Spirit the lens through which to examine more closely the meaning of human life. While we humans are not the only creatures to enjoy life by the power of the Spirit, we do have the capacity for awareness of what it means to be indwelt by God, and thus participate in the life of God even as God breathes through us.

Obviously, more attention could have been devoted to the Spirit's missional task in the world through the church, but many fine texts have taken up that responsibility.6 Much more needs to be said about the Spirit's call for justice, seeking to transform a world plagued by violence and oppression. Further acknowledgement of global threats economically,7 ecologically, and politically could strengthen this text's emphasis on the Spirit's intimate care within this world.8

Each of the chapter titles begins with a gerund as a means of accenting that when we speak of the Spirit, we are preeminently speaking about movement. Never static, the Spirit is God's enlivening action, both within the triune God and encompassing all that God has made. Through vivifying, gathering, empowering, birthing, transforming, winnowing, and honoring, the Spirit forges a partnership between God and all creation that brings both divine and creaturely being to the ultimate realization of participation. Envisioning this goal, Moltmann writes, "Created beings participate in the divine attributes of eternity and omnipresence, just as the indwelling God has participated in their limited time and their restricted space."9 Although we acknowledge that time and eternity are drawn together in the eschatological vision, the mutuality of participation will continue, and the dance will go on.

NOTES

1. Jürgen Moltmann, *The Source of Life: The Holy Spirit and the Theology of Life* (Minneapolis: Fortress, 1997), 131.

2. David S. Cunningham, *These Three Are One: The Practice of Trinitarian Theology* (London: Blackwell, 1998), 165.

3. John V. Taylor, *The Go-Between God: The Holy Spirit and the Christian Mission* (Philadelphia: Fortress, 1973), 179.

4. The best explication of the befriending, sisterly, motherly expressions of the Spirit is that of Elizabeth A. Johnson, *She Who Is: The Mystery of God in Feminist Theological Discourse* (New York: Crossroad, 1992), 144–149.

5. Johnson, *She Who Is*, 149.

6. For example, George R. Hunsberger, *Bearing the Witness of the Spirit: Lesslie Newbigin's Theology of Cultural Plurality* (Grand Rapids: Eerdmans, 1998).

7. Geiko Müller-Fahrenholz writes passionately about the World Council of Churches' attempts to address economic injustice in the world so that a "house of life" might be constructed (*God's Spirit: Transforming a World in Crisis* [New York: Continuum, 1995], 108–112).

8. Lee E. Snook offers significant help in this area in *What in the World Is God Doing? Re-imagining Spirit and Power* (Minneapolis: Fortress, 1999).

9. Jürgen Moltmann, *The Coming of God: Christian Eschatology* (Minneapolis: Fortress, 1996), 307.

BIBLIOGRAPHY

"ABC Leaders Respond to Women's Conference,"
Christian Century 111, no. 11 (April 6 1994): 345.

Alexander, Donald L. *Christian Spirituality: Five Views of
Sanctification.* Downers Grove, IL: InterVarsity Press, 1998.

Allen, Diogenes. *Spiritual Theology: The Theology of Yesterday
for Spiritual Help Today.* Cambridge, Mass.: Cowley
Publications, 1997.

Augustine. *The Enchiridion on Faith, Hope and Love,* trans. J.
F. Shaw, ed. Henry Paolucci. Chicago: Henry Regnery
Gateway, 1961.

Badcock, Gary D. *Light of Truth and Fire of Love: A Theology
of the Holy Spirit.* Grand Rapids: Eerdmans, 1997.

Balz, Horst and Gerhard Schneider. *Exegetical Dictionary of
the New Testament,* vol. 2. Grand Rapids: Eerdmans
Publishing, 1991.

Barbour, Ian G. *When Science Meets Religion: Enemies,
Strangers, or Partners?* New York: HarperCollins, 2000.

Barth, Karl. *The Epistle to the Romans,* trans. Edwyn C.
Hoskyns. London: Oxford University Press, 1933.

Bass, Dorothy C., ed. *Practicing Our Faith: A Way of Life for
a Searching People.* San Francisco: Jossey-Bass Publishers, 1997.

Beasley-Murray, George R. *Baptism in the New Testament.*
London: Paternoster Press, 1962.

Berry, Thomas and Thomas Clarke. *Befriending the Earth:
A Theology of Reconciliation Between Humans and the
Earth.* Mystic, Conn.: Twenty-Third Publications, 1991.

Berry, Thomas. *The Dream of the Earth.* San Francisco: Sierra
Club Books, 1988.

Bettenson, Henry. *Documents of the Christian Church,* 2nd
edition. Oxford: Oxford University Press, 1963.

Boff, Leonardo. *Trinity and Society*, trans. Paul Burns. Maryknoll, N.Y.: Orbis Books, 1988.

Bogart, Dave, ed. *The Bowker Annual: Library and Book Trade Almanac*, 41st edition. New Providence, N.J.: R.R. Bowker, 1996.

Bondi, Robert C. *To Pray and To Love: Conversations on Prayer with the Early Church*. Minneapolis: Fortress, 1991.

Borg, Marcus. *Jesus: A New Vision*. San Francisco, Cal.: Harper and Row, 1987.

Borg, Marcus. *Meeting Jesus Again for the First Time: The Historical Jesus and the Heart of Contemporary Faith*. New York: Harper Collins, 1994.

Breyer, Chloe. *The Close: A Young Woman's First Year at Seminary*. New York: Basic Books, 2000.

Brown, Raymond E., S.S. *The Birth of the Messiah: A Commentary on the Infancy Narratives in Matthew and Luke*. Garden City, N.Y.: Doubleday, 1977.

Brown, Raymond E., S.S. *The Epistles of John*, The Anchor Bible. Garden City, N.Y.: Doubleday, 1982.

Bruggemann, Walter. *Old Testament Theology: Essays on Structure, Theme, and Text*, ed. Patrick D. Miller. Minneapolis: Fortress Press, 1992.

Brueggemann, Walter. *Theology of the Old Testament: Testimony, Dispute, Advocacy*. Minneapolis: Fortress Press, 1997.

Burns, J. Patout and Gerald M. Fagin. *The Holy Spirit*, Message of the Fathers of the Church, 3. Wilmington, Del.: Michael Glazier, 1984.

Burrows, Mark S. "'There the Dance Is': The Dynamics of Spirituality in a Turning World," *American Baptist Quarterly* 16, no. 1 (March 1997): 3–11.

Bynum, Caroline Walker. *The Resurrection of the Body: Western Christianity, 200–1336*. New York: Columbia University Press, 1995.

Cavanaugh, William T. *Torture and Eucharist, Challenges in Contemporary Theology*. Oxford: Blackwell Publishers, 1998.

Charry, Ellen. *By the Renewing of Your Minds: The Pastoral Function of Christian Doctrine*. New York: Oxford University Press, 1997.

Chung Hyun Kyung. "Come, Holy Spirit—Break Down the Walls with Wisdom and Compassion" in *Feminist Theology in the Third World: A Reader*, ed. Ursula King. Maryknoll, N.Y.: Orbis, 1994, 392–394.

Chung Hyun Kyung. "Welcome the Spirit; Hear Her Cries: The Holy Spirit, Creation, and the Culture of Life" *Christianity and Crisis* 51 (July 15, 1991): 220–223.

Comblin, José. *The Holy Spirit and Liberation*. Maryknoll, N.Y.: Orbis Books, 1989.

Congar, Yves. *I Believe in the Holy Spirit*, three vol., trans. David Smith. New York: Crossroad, 1997.

Cox, Harvey. *Fire from Heaven: The Rise of Pentecostal Spirituality and the Reshaping of Religion in the Twenty-first Century*. Reading, Mass.: Addison-Wesley, 1995.

Craddock, Fred B. John Knox Preaching Guides. Atlanta: John Knox Press, 1982.

Culpepper, Robert H. *Evaluating the Charismatic Movement*. Valley Forge: Judson Press, 1977.

Cunningham, David S. *These Three Are One: The Practice of Trinitarian Theology*. Oxford: Blackwell Publishers, 1998.

D'Costa, Gavin. *Sexing the Trinity: Gender, Culture and the Divine*. London: SCM Press, 2000.

Davies, W. D. *Paul and Rabbinic Judaism*, 4th ed. Philadelphia: Fortress, 1980.

Deschner, John. "Legitimating, Limiting, Pluralism" *Christianity and Crisis* 51 (July 15, 1991): 230–232.

Dillard, Annie. *Pilgrim at Tinker Creek*. New York: Harper and Row, 1974.

Donnelly, Doris. *Retrieving Charisms for the Twenty-First Century.* Collegeville, Minn.: Liturgical Press, 1999.

Duck, Ruth C. and Patricia Wilson-Kastner. *Praising God: The Trinity in Christian Worship.* Louisville: Westminster/ John Knox, 1999.

Dunn, James D. G. *The Christ and the Spirit: Collected Essays of James D. G. Dunn,* vol. 2, Pneumatology. Grand Rapids: Eerdmans, 1998.

Elliot, John H. *A Home for the Homeless: A Sociological Exegesis of 1 Peter, Its Situation and Strategy,* rev. ed. Minneapolis: Fortress Press, 1990.

Farris, Patricia. "Bedrock Truths," *Christian Century* 119, no. 3 (January 30–February 6, 2002): 18.

Farrow, Douglas. *Ascension and Ecclesia: On the Significance of the Doctrine of the Ascension for Ecclesiology and Christian Cosmology.* Grand Rapids: Eerdmans, 1999.

Fee, Gordon D. *God's Empowering Presence: The Holy Spirit in the Letters of Paul.* Peabody, Mass.: Hendrickson Publishers, 1994.

Fiddes, Paul S., ed. *Reflections on the Water: Understanding God and the World through the Baptism of Believers,* Regent's Study Guides 4. Macon, Ga.: Smyth and Helwys, 1996.

Finger, Thomas N. *Christian Theology: An Eschatological Approach,* vol. 2. Scottdale, Pa.: Herald Press, 1989.

Floristan, Casiano and Christian Duquoc, eds. *Discernment of the Spirit and of Spirits.* New York: Seabury Press, 1979.

Fox, Matthew. *The Coming of the Cosmic Christ: The Healing of Mother Earth and the Birth of a Global Renaissance.* San Francisco: Harper & Row, 1989.

Fox, Matthew. *Creation Spirituality: Liberating Gifts for the Peoples of the Earth.* San Francisco: Harpers, 1990.

Fox, Matthew. *Original Blessing: A Primer in Creation Spirituality.* Sante Fe, N.M.: Bear and Co., 1983.

Fox, Matthew. *Sins of the Spirit, Blessings of the Flesh: Transforming Evil in Soul and Society.* New York: Three Rivers Press, 1999.

Garland, David E. *Reading Matthew: A Literary and Theological Commentary on the First Gospel.* New York: Crossroad, 1993.

Gaventa, Beverly R. *Mary: Glimpses of the Mother of Jesus.* Minneapolis, Minn.: Fortress Press, 1999.

Gelpi, Donald L., S.J. *The Divine Mother: A Trinitarian Theology of the Holy Spirit.* Lanham, M.D.: University Press of America, 1984.

Gelpi, Donald L., S.J. *Pentecostalism: A Theological Viewpoint.* New York: Paulist Press, 1971.

Gelpi, Donald L., S.J. *The Spirit in the World, Zaccheus Studies: Theology.* Wilmington, Del.: Michael Glazier, 1988.

Gifford, Carolyn De Swarte. "Women in Social Reform Movements" in *Women and Religion in America,* vol. 1, *The Nineteenth Century, A Documentary,* gen. eds. Rosemary Radford Ruether and Rosemary Skinner Keller. San Francisco: Harper and Row, 1981, 294–340.

Gilbert, Olive. *Narrative of Sojourner Truth.* Boston: privately printed, 1875.

"Giving the World a Peek," *U.S. News and World Report,* June 9, 1997, 14.

Goatley, David Emmanuel. "The Improvisation of God: Toward an African American Pneumatology," *Memphis Theological Seminary Journal* 33, no. 1 (spring 1995): 3–13.

Goudey, June Christian. *The Feast of Our Lives: Re-imaging Communion.* Cleveland: The Pilgrim Press, 2002.

Green, Thomas. *Weeds Among the Wheat.* Notre Dame, Ind.: Ave Maria Press, 1984.

Gregory of Nazianzus. "The Fifth Theological Oration: On the Holy Spirit," *Nicene and Post-Nicene Fathers of the Christian Church*, second series, eds. Philip Schaff and Henry Wace. New York: The Christian Literature Company, 1894.

Gregory of Nyssa. *From Glory to Glory: Texts from Gregory of Nyssa's Mystical Writings*, trans. and ed. Herbert Musurillo, S.J. New York: Charles Scribner's Sons, 1961.

Gregory the Great. *Life and Miracles of St. Benedict*, trans. Odo J. Zimmermann, O.S.B. and Benedict R. Avery, O.S.B. Collegeville, Minn.: Liturgical Press, 1949.

Grillmeier, Aloys, S.J. *Christ in Christian Tradition*, vol. I, *From the Apostolic Age to Chalcedon (451)*, second rev. ed, trans. John Bowden. Atlanta: John Knox Press, 1975.

Grudem, Wayne A., ed. *Are Miraculous Gifts for Today?* Grand Rapids: Zondervan Publishing House, 1996.

Gunton, Colin E. *The One, the Three, and the Many: God, Creation, and the Culture of Modernity.* Cambridge: Cambridge University Press, 1993.

Gunton, Colin E. *The Promise of Trinitarian Theology.* Edinburgh: T & T Clark, 1990.

Grenz, Stanley J. *Theology for the Community of God.* Grand Rapids: Eerdmans, 2000.

Hanson, Paul D. *The People Called: The Growth of Community in the Bible.* Louisville: Westminster/John Knox Press, 2001.

Harrison, Verna. "*Perichoresis* in the Greek Fathers," *St. Vladimir's Theological Quarterly* 35, no. 1 (1991): 53–65.

Harvey, Susan Ashbrook. "Feminine Image for the Divine: The Holy Spirit, the Odes of Solomon and Early Syriac Tradition," *St. Vladimir's Theological Quarterly* 37 (1993): 111–139.

Hauerwas, Stanley. "The Sanctified Body: Why Perfection Does Not Require a 'Self'" in *Embodied Holiness: Toward a Corporate Theology of Spiritual Growth*, eds. Samuel M.

Powell and Michael E. Lodahl. Downer's Grove, Ill.:
InterVarsity Press, 1999, 19–38.

Hawthorne, Nathaniel. "The Great Stone Face" in *Greatest
Short Stories*, vol. 1. New York: P.F. Collier, 1953.

Healy, Nicholas M. *Church, World and the Christian Life:
Practical-Prophetic Ecclesiology*, Cambridge Studies in Christian Doctrine. Cambridge: Cambridge University Press, 2000.

Heim, S. Mark. *Salvations: Truth and Difference in Religion*.
Maryknoll: Orbis Books, 1995.

Hendry, George. *The Holy Spirit in Christian Theology*. London:
SCM Press, 1957.

Hengel, Martin. *The Son of God: The Origin of Christology
and the History of Jewish-Hellenistic Religion*, trans. John
Bowden. Philadelphia: Fortress, 1976.

Heron, Alasdair I. C. *The Holy Spirit: The Holy Spirit in the
Bible, the History of Christian Thought, and Recent
Theology*. Philadelphia: Westminster Press, 1983.

Hodgson, Peter C. *God in History: Shapes of Freedom*.
Nashville: Abingdon Press, 1989.

Hodgson, Peter C. *Winds of the Spirit: A Constructive Christian Theology*. Louisville: Westminster/John Knox Press, 1994.

Hollenweger, Walter J. *The Pentecostals*. London: SCM Press,
1972.

Horsley, Richard A. and Neil Asher Silberman. *The Message
and the Kingdom: How Jesus and Paul Ignited a Revolution
and Transformed the Ancient World*. Minneapolis: Fortress
Press, 1997.

Hunsberger, George R. *Bearing the Witness of the Spirit:
Lesslie Newbigin's Theology of Cultural Plurality*. Grand
Rapids: Eerdmans, 1998.

Isherwood, Lisa. *Introducing Feminist Christologies,
Introductions in Feminist Theology*. Cleveland: The Pilgrim
Press, 2002.

James, Robison B. "Beyond Old Habits and on to a New Land," in *Beyond the Impasse: Scripture, Interpretation, and Theology in Baptist Life*, eds. Robison B. James and David S. Dockery. Nashville: Broadman Press, 1992, 118–148.

Jensen, Robin Margaret. *Understanding Early Christian Art*. New York: Routledge, 2000.

Jenson, Robert W. "The Great Transformation" in *The Last Things: Biblical and Theological Perspectives on Eschatology*, eds. Carl E. Braaten and Robert W. Jenson. Grand Rapids: Eerdmans, 2002, 33–42.

Johnson, Elizabeth A. *She Who Is: The Mystery of God in Feminist Theological Discourse*. New York: Crossroad, 1992.

Johnson, Elizabeth A. *Women, Earth, and Creator Spirit*. Mahwah, N.J.: Paulist Press, 1993.

Johnson, Luke Timothy. *Scripture and Discernment: Decision Making in the Church*. Nashville: Abingdon Press, 1996.

King, Martin Luther, Jr. *Stride Toward Freedom*. New York: Harper and Row, 1958.

Kinnamon, Michael, ed. *Signs of the Spirit: Official Report, Seventh Assembly.* Geneva: World Council of Churches, 1991.

Kishkovsky, Leonid. "Ecumenical Journey: Authentic Dialogue." *Christianity and Crisis* 51 (July 15, 1991): 228–229.

Kuschel, Karl-Josef. *Born Before All Time?: The Dispute Over Christ's Origin*, trans. John Bowden. London: SCM Press, 1992.

LaCugna, Catherine Mowry. *God For Us: The Trinity and the Christian Life*. San Francisco: HarperCollins, 1991.

Lathrop, Gordon W. *Holy Things: A Liturgical Theology.* Minneapolis: Fortress, 1993.

LaVerdiere, Eugene, S.S.S. *The Eucharist in the New Testament and the Early Church*. Collegeville, Minn.: Liturgical Press, 1996.

Lawler, Michael G. "*Perichoresis:* New Theological Wine in An Old Theological Wineskin," *Horizons* 22, no. 1 (1995): 49–66.

Lefebure, Leo D. "The Wisdom of God: Sophia and Christian Theology," *Christian Century* 111, no. 29 (October 19, 1994): 951.

Levertov, Denise. *The Stream and the Sapphire: Selected Poems on Religious Themes.* New York: New Directions Publishing, 1997.

Lewis, C. S. *Till We Have Faces: A Myth Retold.* New York: Harcourt, Brace and Company, 1956.

Liddell, Henry and Robert Scott. *Greek-English Lexicon.* Oxford: Clarendon, 1980.

Lodahl, Michael E. *Shekinah/Spirit: Divine Presence in Jewish and Christian Religion.* New York: Paulist Press, 1992.

Luther, Martin. *Heidelberg Thesis.* (1518).

Luther, Martin. *Luther's Works,* vol. 40., ed. Conrad Bergendoff. Philadelphia: Fortress Press, 1958.

Malina, Bruce. *The Social Gospel of Jesus: The Kingdom of God in Mediterranean Perspective.* Minneapolis: Fortress Press, 2001.

Maloney, George A., S.J. *The Spirit Broods Over the World.* New York: Alba House, 1993.

Marsh, Thomas. *The Triune God: A Biblical, Historical, and Theological Study.* Mystic, Conn.: Twenty-Third Publications, 1994.

Marshall, Molly T. "The Changing Face of Baptist Discipleship," *Review and Expositor* 95, no. 1 (winter 1998): 59–73.

Marshall, Molly T. "The Fullness of Incarnation: God's New Humanity in the Body of Christ," *Review and Expositor* 93, no. 2 (spring 1996): 187–201.

Marshall, Molly T. *No Salvation Outside the Church? A Critical Inquiry.* Lewiston: Edwin Mellen, 1993.

Marshall, Molly T. "Spiritual Formation: Humanity as Unfinished Presence," *Freedom of Conscience*, ed. Paul D. Simmons. Amherst, N.Y.: Prometheus Press, 2000, 194–203.

Martin, Ralph P. *Carmen-Christi: Philippians 2:5-11 in Recent Interpretation and in the Setting of Early Christian Worship*, rev. ed. Grand Rapids: Eerdmans, 1983.

McClendon, James Wm., Jr. *Systematic Theology: Doctrine*, vol. 2. Nashville: Abingdon Press, 1994.

McDonnell, Kilian. "The Determinative Doctrine of the Holy Spirit," *Theology Today* 39 no. 2 (July 1982): 142–161.

McDonnell, Kilian. "A Trinitarian Theology of the Holy Spirit?" *Theological Studies* 46 (1985): 191-227.

McFague, Sallie. *The Body of God: An Ecological Theology*. Minneapolis: Fortress Press, 1993.

McGill, Arthur C. *Suffering: A Test of Theological Method*. Philadelphia: Westminster Press, 1968.

McIntyre, John. *The Shape of Pneumatology: Studies in the Doctrine of the Holy Spirit*. Edinburgh: T & T Clark, 1997.

Miles, Margaret R. *Practicing Christianity: Critical Perspectives for an Embodied Spirituality*. New York: Crossroad, 1990.

Miller, Sara. "Global Gospel," *Christian Century* 119, no. 15 (July 17–30, 2002), 20–27.

Mills, Watson E., ed. *Speaking in Tongues: Let's Talk About It*. Waco: Word Books, 1973.

Moltmann, Jürgen. *The Coming of God: Christian Eschatology*. Minneapolis, Minn.: Fortress Press, 1996.

Moltmann, Jürgen. *Experiences in Theology: Ways and Forms of Christian Theology*, trans. Margaret Kohl. Minneapolis, Minn.: Fortress, 2000.

Moltmann, Jürgen. *History and the Triune God: Contributions to Trinitarian Theology*, trans. John Bowden. New York: Crossroad, 1992.

Moltmann, Jürgen. *The Source of Life: The Holy Spirit and the Theology of Life*. Minneapolis, Minn.: Fortress Press, 1997.

Moltmann, Jürgen. *The Spirit of Life: A Universal Affirmation*, trans. Margaret Kohl. Minneapolis, Minn.: Fortress Press, 1992.

Moltmann, Jürgen. *The Trinity and the Kingdom: The Doctrine of God*, trans. Margaret Kohl. San Francisco: Harper and Row, 1981.

Moltmann, Jürgen. *The Way of Jesus Christ: Christology in Messianic Dimensions*, trans. Margaret Kohl. San Francisco: HarperSanFrancisco, 1990.

Montague, George T. *Holy Spirit: Growth of a Biblical Tradition*. Peabody, Mass.: Hendrickson Publishers, 1976.

Moody, Dale. *Baptism: Foundation for Christian Unity*. Philadelphia: Westminster Press, 1967.

Moody, Dale. *Spirit of the Living God: The Biblical Concepts Interpreted in Context*. Philadelphia: Westminster Press, 1968.

Morris, Danny E. and Charles M. Olsen. *Discerning God's Will Together: A Spiritual Practice for the Church*. Nashville: Upper Room Books, 1997.

Morse, Christopher. *Not Every Spirit: A Dogmatics of Christian Disbelief*. Valley Forge, Pa.: Trinity Press International, 1994.

Müller-Fahrenholz, Geiko. *God's Spirit: Transforming a World in Crisis*. New York: Continuum, 1995.

Navone, John, S.J. *Self-giving and Sharing: The Trinity and Human Fulfillment*. Collegeville, Minn.: Liturgical Press, 1989.

Newman, Carey C. *Paul's Glory-Christology: Tradition and Rhetoric*. Leiden: E. J. Brill, 1992.

Neyrey, Jerome H., ed. *The Social World of Luke-Acts: Models for Interpretation*. Peabody, Mass.: Hendrickson, 1991.

Ngong Tonghou David. "Left Behind," *Theology Today* 59 (July 2002), 285–286.

Nouwen, Henri J. M. *Behold the Beauty of the Lord: Praying with Icons.* Notre Dame, Ind.: Ave Maria Press, 1987.

Oates, Wayne E. *The Holy Spirit and Contemporary Man.* Grand Rapids: Baker Book House, 1974.

Pannenberg, Wolfhart. "The Doctrine of the Spirit and the Task of a Theology of Nature," *Theology* 75, no. 619 (January 1972): 8–21.

Pannenberg, Wolfhart. *Systematic Theology,* vol. 1, trans. Geoffrey W. Bromiley. Grand Rapids: Eerdmans, 1991.

Pannenberg, Wolfhart. *Systematic Theology,* vol. 2, trans. Geoffrey W. Bromiley. Grand Rapids: Eerdmans, 1991.

Pascal, Blaise. *Pensées,* trans. A.J. Krailsheimer. New York: Penguin Books, 1966.

Paulsell, Stephanie. "Honoring the Body" in *Practicing Our Faith,* ed. Dorothy C. Bass. San Francisco: Jossey-Bass Publishers, 1997, 13–27.

Peters, Ted. *GOD as Trinity: Relationality and Temporality in Divine Life.* Louisville: Westminster/John Knox Press, 1993.

Pittenger, Norman. *The Holy Spirit.* Philadelphia: United Church Press, 1974.

Pohl, Christine D. *Making Room: Recovering Hospitality as a Christian Tradition.* Grand Rapids: Eerdmans, 1999.

Polkinghorne, John, ed. *The Work of Love: Creation as Kenosis.* Grand Rapids: Eerdmans, 2001.

Prichard, Rebecca Button. *Sensing the Spirit: The Holy Spirit in Feminist Perspective.* St. Louis: Chalice Press, 1999.

Primavesi, Anne. *From Apocalypse to Genesis: Ecology, Feminism and Christianity.* Minneapolis: Fortress Press, 1991.

Rahner, Karl, S.J. "Anonymous Christians" in *Theological Investigations,* vol. 6, trans. Karl H. Kruger and Boniface Kruger. Baltimore: Helicon Press, 1969.

Reynolds, Blair. *Toward a Process Pneumatology.* London and Toronto: Associated University Presses, 1990.

Robinson, John A. T. *The Body: A Study in Pauline Theology.* Philadelphia: Westminster Press, 1952.

Robinson, John A. T. *The Human Face of God.* Philadelpia: Westminster Press, 1973.

Rogers, Frank, Jr. "Discernment" in *Practicing Our Faith*, ed. Dorothy C. Bass. San Francisco: Jossey-Bass Publishers, 1997, 105–118.

Ruether, Rosemary Radford. *Gaia and God: An Ecofeminist Theology of Earth Healing.* New York: HarperSanFrancisco, 1992.

Rupp, George. *Commitment and Community.* Minneapolis, Minn.: Fortress Press, 1989.

Russell, Letty. *Church in the Round: Feminist Interpretation of the Church.* Louisville: Westminster/John Knox, 1993.

Saliers, Don E. "Singing Our Lives" in *Practicing Our Faith*, ed. Dorothy C. Bass. San Francisco: Jossey-Bass, 1997, 179–193.

Saliers, Don E. *Worship Come to Its Senses.* Nashville: Abingdon, 1996.

Scholem, Gershom. *Major Trends in Jewish Mysticism.* New York: Schocken Books, Inc., 1995.

Schüssler Fiorenza, Elizabeth. *Discipleship of Equals: A Critical Feminist Ekklesialogy of Liberation.* New York: Crossroad, 1993.

Schüssler Fiorenza, Elizabeth. *In Memory of Her: A Feminist Reconstruction of Christian Origins.* New York: Crossroad, 1983.

Schüssler Fiorenza, Elizabeth. *JESUS, Miriam's Child, Sophia's Prophet: Critical Issues in Feminist Christology.* New York: Continuum, 1994.

Sherry, Patrick. *Spirit and Beauty: An Introduction to Theological Aesthetics.* Oxford: Clarendon Press, 1992.

Simon, Ulrich. *A Theology of Auschwitz.* London: SPCK, 1978.

Sittler, Joseph. *Gravity and Grace: Reflections and Provocations*, ed. Linda-Marie Delloff. Minneapolis, Minn.: Augsburg, 1986.

Small, Joseph D. and John P. Burgess. "Evaluating 'Re-Imagining'," *Christian Century* 111, no. 11 (April 6, 1994): 342–344.

Smith, Dennis E. and Hal E. Taussig. *Many Tables: The Eucharist in the New Testament and Liturgy Today.* Philadelphia: Trinity Press International, 1990.

Smith, Kenneth L. and Ira G. Zepp Jr. *Search for the Beloved Community: The Thinking of Martin Luther King, Jr.* Valley Forge, Pa.: Judson Press, 1988.

Snook, Lee E. *What In the World Is God Doing? Re-imagining Spirit and Power.* Minneapolis, Minn.: Fortress, 1999.

Staaniloae, Dumitru. *Theology and the Church*, trans. Robert Barringer. Crestwood, N.Y.: St. Vladimir's Seminary Press, 1980.

Stacy, R. Wayne. "Baptism" in *A Baptist's Theology*, ed. R. Wayne Stacy. Macon: Smyth and Helwys, 1999, 152–174.

Stagg, Frank. *The Holy Spirit Today.* Nashville: Broadman, 1973.

Stevenson, J. and W. H. C. Frend, ed. *Creeds, Councils, and Controversies*, rev. ed. London: SPCK, 1989.

Stookey, Laurence Hull. *Baptism: Christ's Act in the Church.* Nashville: Abingdon, 1982.

Stookey, Laurence Hull. *Eucharist: Christ's Feast with the Church.* Nashville: Abingdon Press, 1993.

Suchocki, Majorie. "Theological Foundations for Ethnic and Gender Diversity in Faculties or Excellence and the Motley Crew," *Theological Education* 26, no. 2 (spring 1990): 35–50.

Tanner, Kathryn. *Jesus, Humanity, and the Trinity: A Brief Systematic Theology.* Minneapolis, Minn.: Fortress Press, 2001.

Taylor, John V. *The Go-Between God: The Holy Spirit and the Christian Mission.* New York: Oxford University Press, 1972.

Taylor, Mark C. *Erring: A Postmodern A/theology.* Chicago: University of Chicago Press, 1984.

Terrien, Samuel. "The Elusive Presence: Toward a New Biblical Theology," *Religious Perspectives,* vol. 26. San Francisco: Harper and Row, 1978.

Thiemann, Ronald F. *Revelation and Theology: The Gospel as Narrated Promise.* Notre Dame, Ind.: University of Notre Dame Press, 1985.

Thomas Aquinas. *Nature and Grace: Selections from the* Summa Theologica *of Thomas Aquinas,* trans. and ed. A. M. Fairweather. Philadelphia: Westminster Press, 1954.

Thomas Aquinas. *Summa Theologica,* in *The Great Books of the Western World,* trans. Fathers of the English Dominican Province, rev. Daniel J. Sullivan. Chicago: Encyclopedia Britannica, Inc., 1952.

Torbet, Robert G. *A History of the Baptists,* 3rd ed. Valley Forge, Pa.: Judson Press, 1973.

Torrance, James B. *Worship, Community and the Triune God of Grace.* Downers Grove, Ill.: InterVarsity Press, 1996.

Torrance, T. F. *Space, Time, and Resurrection.* Grand Rapids: Eerdmans, 1976.

Townes, Emilie M. *Embracing the Spirit: Womanist Perspectives on Hope, Salvation, and Transformation.* Maryknoll: Orbis Books, 1997.

Trible, Phyllis. "Bringing Miriam Out of the Shadows," *Bible Review* 5 (Fall 1989): 14–25, 34.

Trible, Phyllis. *God and the Rhetoric of Sexuality.* Philadelphia: Fortress Press, 1978.

Ubi Caritas, text: Latin, 9th c., trans. by Richard Proulx, GIA Publications.

Vickery, Jeffrey D. "Light from the East: Asian Contributions to Contemporary North American Theology." Unpublished dissertation, The Southern Baptist Theological Seminary, Louisville, 1996.

Volf, Miroslav. *After Our Likeness: The Church as the Image of the Trinity.* Grand Rapids: Eerdmans, 1998.

Volf, Miroslav. *Exclusion and Embrace: A Theological Exploration of Identity, Otherness, and Reconciliation.* Nashville: Abingdon, 1996.

Wallace, Mark I. *Fragments of the Spirit: Nature, Violence, and the Renewal of Creation.* New York: Continuum, 1996.

Weil, Simone. *Waiting for God.* New York: Harper and Row, 1951.

Welker, Michael. *God the Spirit*, trans. John F. Hoffmeyer. Minneapolis, Minn.: Fortress Press, 1994.

Welker, Michael. *What Happens in Holy Communion?* Grand Rapids: Eerdmans, 2000.

West, Cornel. *Race Matters.* Boston: Beacon Press, 1993.

Williams, Rowan. *Writing in the Dust: After September 11.* Grand Rapids: Eerdmans, 2002.

Willimon, William H. "Vocational Temptation," *Theology Today* 52, no. 1 (April 1995): 98–101.

Wink, Walter. *Naming the Powers: The Language of Power in the New Testament.* Philadelphia: Westminster Press, 1984.

Wilson-Kastner, Patricia. *Faith, Feminism, and the Christ.* Philadelphia: Fortress, 1983.

Wolff, Hans Walter. *Anthropology of the Old Testament.* Philadelphia: Fortress, 1975.

Wootton, Janet. *Introducing a Practical Feminist Theology of Worship, Introductions in Feminist Theology.* Cleveland: The Pilgrim Press, 2000.

Wren, Brian. *Bring Many Names.* Carol Stream, Ill.: Hope Publishing Company, 1989.

Wren, Brian. *Praying Twice: The Music and Words of Congregational Song*. Louisville: Westminster/John Knox Press, 2000.

Wright, Wendy M. "Contemplation in Time of War," *Weaving* 7, no. 4 (July/August 1992): 16–27.

Wright, Wendy M. "Living into the Image," *Weavings*, Vol. 12, no. 1 (January/February), 1997: 6–17.

Wuthnow, Robert. *After Heaven: Spirituality in America Since the 1950s*. Berkeley and Los Angeles: University of California Press, 1998.

Zikmund, Barbara Brown. "Feminist Consciousness in Historical Perspective" in *Feminist Interpretation of the Bible*, ed. Letty M. Russell. Philadelphia: Westminster Press, 1985, 21–29.

Zizioulas, John. *Being as Communion*. Crestwood, N.Y.: St. Vladimir's Seminary Press, 1985.

SCRIPTURE INDEX